I Ching Decision Maker

I Ching Decision Maker

Kim Farnell

A Sterling / Zambezi Book

Sterling Publishing Co., Inc.

New York

Library of Congress Cataloging-in-Publication Data Available

2   4   6   8   10   9   7   5   3   1

Published in 2004 by
Sterling Publishing Co., Inc.
387 Park Avenue South
New York, NY 10016

Published and distributed in the UK soley by
Zambezi Publishing Limited
P.O. Box 221 Plymouth,
Devon PL2 2YJ (UK)

Distributed in Canada by Sterling Publishing
c/o Canadian Manda Group
165 Dufferin Street
Toronto, Ontario, Canada M6K 3H6

Distributed in Australia by Capricorn Link (Australia) Pty Ltd.
P.O. Box 704, Windsor, NSW 2756, Australia

Typesetting by Zambezi Publishing, Plymouth, UK

Sterling ISBN 1-4027-1222-7
Zambezi ISBN 1-903065-32-1

Contents

What Is the I Ching?

The I Ching, or Book of Changes, is an ancient Chinese oracle that can be consulted for its philosophy, advice, and for divination. If you need to make a decision or solve a problem, you can consult the I Ching to gain a better understanding of your present and future situation. You start by working through a procedure that produces a six-line pattern called a hexagram. Then you find your hexagram in the illustration, locate its number, and read the interpretation.

This ancient book blends the principles of astronomy and astrology to give a comprehensive text that covers ideas, images, and natural laws. It describes an ancient system that is at the heart of Chinese cultural beliefs. The philosophy centers on the idea of balance through the opposite concepts of accepting a given situation or working to change it. The I Ching represents one of man's earliest efforts to grasp his relationship with nature and the society in which he lives. This ancient book of wisdom suggests the correct and balanced action that should be taken in any one of a multitude of situations. The basis of the I Ching philosophy is that nothing is static, so our task is to adjust to the ebb and flow of changing circumstances. A mix of Taoist and Confucian philosophy that has evolved over many centuries, the I Ching may be the oldest book in existence.

The Hexagrams

The book contains a series of hexagrams, each of which consists of six lines. Any or all of the six lines may have a gap in them, or they may be complete. The lines represent the two primal principles of yang and yin. Yang is the active, energetic, masculine principle and yin is the passive, nurturing, feminine principle. The unbroken lines represent yang and the broken ones represent yin. Each hexagram is linked to a piece of advice that throws light on a problem and provides useful information. When all the combinations of broken or unbroken lines are written down, the total possible number comes to 64. Each of the 64 hexagrams represents a process or change that is happening at the time of consultation.

The Trigrams and the Hexagrams

A trigram is a pattern of three lines, any of which may be solid or broken. A hexagram consists of two trigrams, one atop the other.

Lower / Inner Trigram   **Upper / Outer Trigram**

Hexagram

In the West, we are accustomed to writing across and down the page, but the trigrams and hexagrams are created by starting at the bottom and working upwards. The first trigram forms the bottom half of the hexagram, while the second trigram is placed on top. When analyzing the I Ching, the three lines in the *lower* trigram are seen as the *inner aspect* of the change that is occurring, while the three lines in the *upper* trigram refer to its *outer aspect*. The inner aspect means the way you feel about something and the actions that you are taking; the outer aspect involves any outside influences. This means that you can use both the hexagram and trigram chapters in this book to throw light on your situation.

The I Ching can help you to make decisions that logic alone cannot handle and to reduce the stress that arises when you find it hard to make up your mind. It will enable you to manage sensitive relationships more successfully, to develop better timing, and to access your creative insight and intuitive power.

The choices that we make on a daily basis determine our level of success, but when a crisis or an emotional situation occurs, logic alone becomes inadequate—if not impossible. It is only by tapping into our own intuitive resources that we can find the answers. When we have a problem, no matter what decision we come to, it is all too easy for us to fear that our decision is the wrong one. This anxiety makes it more difficult for us to be receptive to a resolution, but our dilemmas can be made easier to solve with the help of the I Ching.

Consulting the I Ching is different to using runes or Tarot cards, because it does not foretell the future as much as make a situation clearer. It relies on the fact that achieving good fortune and avoiding misfortune depends on the choices that we make, so it does not remove the element of free will. When we consult the I Ching, we are not passively accepting our destiny; we are actively creating our own fortune. If our actions are in keeping with the advice of the I Ching, our fortune will be good. If our actions are out of harmony with the counsel, or if we refuse to act when action is called for, then our fortune will be bad.

The hexagrams embody many layers of meaning, so if you wish to reap the oracle's full benefit, you will need to think and to use your intuition. After a while, revelations will spring up from your unconscious mind, so it will take practice before you become truly skilled at making use of the interpretations.

Changing Lines

We know that the words *I Ching* mean "Book of Changes," and it is obvious that the "changes" are the situations that face us during the course of our lives. However, there is a more practical form of change that is characteristic of the I Ching. The lines in a hexagram pattern can be made to change, thereby giving you a second hexagram reading. If you happen to come up with a hexagram that changes its character, this indicates to you that your current situation has neared its limit and that it will soon change to something else. The I Ching then gives a further reading that offers insight into future trends.

This Book in Particular

It is actually quite difficult to reconcile the language, ideas, and moods of the I Ching with Western preoccupations. Some translations offer a glimpse of the poetry of the original Chinese scripts, and this can make their style appear archaic. I have tried to avoid taking a bludgeon to the poetic nature of the I Ching, while also making it accessible and useful to a modern reader.

The second problem is that Chinese preoccupations do not appear to be the same as ours. This is especially so when one considers the attitudes and lifestyle of the educated Chinese people who wrote these texts so long ago. Many of the comments have an underlying theme of maintaining "face" or status and of not attracting scorn or mockery. Other ideas are of persistence, patience, and of keeping going in the face of adversity. This does not quite gel with modern Western notions of independence, of demanding our right to happiness, and of giving up as soon as a problem appears to be intractable. However, when one gives a little thought to these concepts, how many of us would enjoy looking stupid, unfashionable, out of touch, or incapable? In addition, how many of us have to keep going at times when life grinds us down or throws a wrench into the works? Perhaps these ideas of fitting in with the prevailing order when needs be, of appearing to be in control of the circumstances that we find ourselves in, and of seeing things through to their conclusion are not silly after all?

Don't Ignore the Images

When you reach the interpretation chapter, you will see the names for the two trigrams that make up each hexagram, and also brief sections for each hexagram that are entitled "The Image." Don't skip over these in your haste to reach the interpretation, because the images are powerful metaphors for what is going on in your life and for what the I Ching is trying to tell you.

In the West, we have many sayings that derive from weather and topography. Consider: *"go with the flow, no smoke without fire, cannot see the wood for the trees, it never rains but it pours,"* and so on. The Chinese are a rural people, most of whom live inland. For many millennia they have struggled to cope with nature, so they are familiar with geographic and meteorological images that stand as metaphors for life. Images such as a calm lake, an impassable abyss, the stillness of a mountain, a campfire that gives light and warmth on one hand, but which destroys trees while it rages through a forest on the other, are easy to understand.

Following are a couple of examples; you will see many more when you reach the hexagram chapter. A river that is narrowed between two high banks becomes a torrent, and thus a symbol of danger. For us, thunder is frightening and dangerous, but to the Chinese it signals the end of a hard, frozen winter, heralding the start of summer and warm irrigating rain, so it is a welcome sign of change for the better.

As mentioned earlier, each hexagram is composed of two trigrams placed one above the other. The trigrams contain powerful images. For example: heaven, earth, thunder, water, wind, wood, mountain, fire, marsh, lake, river, and so on. It is the juxtaposition of these images (one above the other) that creates the individual design of each hexagram and its individual meaning.

Consider the image of a lake (lake = first image) tucked into the upper reaches of a mountain (mountain = second image). The lake overflows from time to time and dribbles down to irrigate the mountain, thereby making its lower slopes fertile. This is a welcome image, which creates a beneficial hexagram. So, use these images as we ourselves do every day of our lives. Then you will not allow the tide of events to overtake you, the winds of change to buffet you while you keep your feet on the ground and try to move mountains.

Don't Ignore the Keywords Either

When you scan through the section marked "Keywords," certain words will spring out and connect with what is going on in your life. These keywords will jumpstart your intuition as to what is happening, what is to come, and what you should do about it.

The History of the I Ching

The I Ching is the most widely read of the five Chinese Classics. Although there are many theories, no one knows exactly when it was written. Although there are many theories, no one knows exactly when it was written. Although the ideas behind the I Ching may seem confusing and esoteric to us, it is revered by the educated men and women of the East. The I Ching is a mix of Taoist and Confucian philosophy, which has evolved over the centuries. There are two histories of the I Ching: the practical and the mythological—and neither is certain.

The Academic View

It is thought that the I Ching developed out of tortoise shell and ox shoulder bone divination. A red-hot stone was applied to ox bones, and the random pattern of cracks that appeared was examined by priests who deduced their meaning. Ancient Chinese soothsayers looked for portents in the cracks of tortoise shells that were heated over a fire and then doused with water. The geometric patterns made by the resulting cracks were then studied for the wisdom that they were thought to contain. This system gradually developed into a method involving the division of yarrow stalks, then into coin tossing, and finally the practices of modern I Ching.

In China, the patterns of cracks inspired a systematic approach in terms of geometric lines—the hexagrams.

Exactly how the jump from cracks to hexagrams was made is unknown. The trigrams were added later.

The mythological view

Thousands of years ago—about 2852–2738 B.C.—there lived the Chinese sage and first Emperor of China known as Fu Hsi. He was responsible for recording many agricultural and engineering ideas and for bringing ethics and civilized conduct into the world. His ethical texts were translated into memorable verses, and some of these became absorbed into the I Ching. One day, he saw the dragon-headed tortoise, or Lo Shu, rise from the Yangtze River. On its side were markings, which he recorded as a map. Using these lines, he derived the first trigrams. The primary principles, the yin and yang, were linked to two primary trigrams. These were each split into four images that were then used to generate the total of eight possible trigrams.

Over time and in stages, the incredibly clever Fu Hsi created the sixty-four Kua of the I Ching. Fu Hsi surveyed all the movements under heaven. He saw the ways the movements met and became interrelated, and he learned the way their courses were governed by eternal laws. He thought through the order of nature to its deepest core. He perceived the beginning of all things that lay unmoving in the beyond, and in so doing he arrived at an understanding of fate.

Much later, another mythical emperor, Yu, saw a tortoise with similar markings on its shell rising from the Lo River. This became the Lo Shu Map. Yu interpreted the four directions and four diagonal directions of the Lo Shu in terms of the Later Heaven (asymmetrical) arrangement of the eight trigrams of the I Ching, and he incorporated the four seasons and five elements. These teachings were handed down orally, with each generation educating the next. When writing began in China, the I Ching teachings and answers were recorded on pieces of bamboo, and so the I Ching and its teachings flourished.

Wen Wang (1150 B.C.) is thought to have been the creator of the present hexagrams. He was a powerful feudal lord who angered the Emperor, Chou Hsin. Chou Hsin was the last emperor of the Shang Dynasty, and a cruel and heartless man who tortured people to please his equally sadistic concubine. He was so cruel that all China lived in fear of him.

Wen was a scholar who governed a small province in a remote area of western China. He governed his people according to I Ching principles, and he was as loved and respected by the people as Chou Hsin was hated and feared. The people urged Wen to gather an army and overthrow the tyrant, assuring him that everyone would willingly follow him. He refused, saying that, since he was a truly law abiding citizen, he could not in all conscience take action against his emperor. Chou Hsin heard the rumors that Wen was being asked to gather an army to rise against him and he ordered Wen to be put in prison. Wen was allowed to live, but only because of his popularity.

While Wen was in confinement and in fear for his life, he used the I Ching's wisdom and its divinatory powers to maintain his courage. At this time, there were two versions of the I Ching: the Lien Sah and the Gai Tsen. While Wen was in prison, he reinterpreted the names of the Kua and other parts of the great books. He also changed the order of the Kua that had been established by Fu Hsi to the order currently in use. It is said that he did this as a result of a vision that he saw on the wall of his prison. After Wen had been in prison for a year, influential friends arranged for him to be freed.

In 1122 B.C., Wen's eldest son, Yu, publicly denounced Emperor Chou Hsin and gathered together an army to overthrow the tyrant. When he became king, Yu honored his then—deceased father by bestowing upon him the title of King. Wen was forever after known as King Wen, although he had never actually ruled as king in his lifetime. King Yu died

a few years later, leaving his thirteen-year-old son as heir to
the throne. As he was so young, Chou Hsin's son, Tan, who
was known as the Duke of Chou, ruled in his stead. It seems
that Tan was a very different type of man from his father. King
Wen had already instructed Tan in the teachings of the I
Ching, but it was Tan who moved the I Ching forward by
interpreting the meanings of the individual lines. The I Ching
was then considered complete. In 1109 B.C. the book became
known as the Chou I—"The Changes of Chou."

Several hundred more years passed. In the fifth century
B.C., Kung Fu-Tze came onto the world scene. This was the
great sage and scholar whom we know as Confucius.
Confucius studied the Chou I and he wrote many
commentaries on the Book of Changes. His work was
incorporated into the Confucian canon as the I Ching—the
Book (or Classic) of Changes. Confucius made it one of the
most popular forms of oracular divination in China. Later
scholars blended principles of astronomy and Chinese
astrology (the twelve signs and the five elements) into the I
Ching. Some people believe that the I Ching is a completely
Confucist document, and that it is one of the five Confucian
Classics, but this is an unlikely notion, however romantic. In
the years to come, other sages and scholars added to the study
of the I Ching, until the eight trigrams were developed into the
sixty-four hexagrams, each with its own name, attributes, and
commentaries.

After this time, many philosophies proliferated and
different versions and interpretations of the I Ching abounded.
Much later, the Emperor Chin unified China and gave it a
strong government. To keep control, he outlawed scholarly
knowledge, including the works of Confucius. However, the I
Ching survived by being passed on through oral tradition.
During the last Imperial dynasty, from 1644 to 1912, the
original roots of the I Ching were rediscovered and studied.
The communist government that came into being in 1949
disapproved of Chinese divination, believing it to be useless

superstition. However, this time round it was impossible to ban the I Ching because it was so widely known, and printed versions existed in many places outside China.

The I Ching made its debut in France in the early eighteenth century. It did not gain popularity until the late nineteenth century, when a German Christian missionary called Richard Wilhelm translated it. Since then it has grown steadily in popularity in the West until the present time.

Casting the I Ching

Asking Your Question

The I Ching cannot be used to give an overview of the future in the way that the Tarot can because it is geared for answering specific questions. It is worth spending some time defining your question, perhaps noting it down on paper in order to clarify it. You may wish to add comments about the circumstances surrounding your question. This not only helps you to formulate your question, but it is useful for you to refer to later, especially while you are still learning. Secondly, the I Ching does not always give a straight yes or no answer. It offers guidance as to what the results of a certain course of action are likely to be. For example, you might ask: "What can I expect if I accept the job that I have been offered?"

If you note down the date, time, and location of each question alongside the answer, you will start to build up an invaluable resource. Look back to your questions and answers from time to time to see what happened.

Casting Methods

The simplest form of casting is to use three coins. If you wish, you can buy copies of ancient Chinese coins in a gift shop and then keep these for your I Ching readings. Alternatively, ask your bank to give you three shiny new coins of any currency. It is best to use three coins of the same denomination, as they will be the same size and weight. It is also best to use new coins, as these will have fewer stray "vibes" left on them by those who have used them as currency. If you use Chinese coins, you will need to choose which side will represent heads to you and which will be tails, as this is not immediately clear to a Westerner. Whatever coins you use, keep them aside and use them specifically for your I Ching readings. To give your readings a touch of ceremony, keep a small cloth aside for the purpose, placing it on the table before throwing your coins.

When you throw three coins, they will land as three of a kind or two of one kind and one of the other. If the majority of the coins land as heads, this indicates yang. If the majority land as tails, it indicates yin. There is a difference between an answer that is arrived at when all three coins land with the same side up to that which is arrived at by a majority of two heads or two tails. The Chinese add complications to this, but in this book we will keep the system simple. Each throw creates one line of the hexagram, so six throws give you the full hexagram.

Another traditional method of casting the I Ching is by using yarrow stalks. Fifty stalks are used in a complicated ritual of counting, dividing them, and slotting certain sticks between certain fingers. There is less likelihood of arriving at a completely yang or yin answer when using yarrow sticks, as this does tend to give a more yang—and thus more positive—answer. This is also very difficult to do properly.

One recent innovation is the use of marbles. This method is designed to be quick, while also giving the same mathematical probabilities as the yarrow stalk method. For this, you need sixteen marbles, eight each of two different colors. Designate half the marbles to represent yang and half to represent yin. Place your marbles in a bag, then remove one marble at a time, note down whether it represents yang or yin, and replace it in the bag. Continue until you have all six lines of the hexagram. However, for this book, I will keep to the coin method.

Starting Out

Meditate on your question, and hold the question in your mind. Throw the coins gently up into the air while still thinking of your question. If the majority of coins are yang (heads), draw a straight line.

If the majority of the coins are yin (tails), draw a line with a break in it.

If you have thrown three heads or three tails, draw a little cross in the middle of your line. This special line will become important later when we start to look at lines that change.

Once you have done this, repeat the process, but draw your second line above the first. Then do the same four more times, drawing each new line above the last—until you have a total of six lines. You will end up with something like the example below.

The hexagram as a whole has a meaning, but so do the three lower and the three upper lines in the design, as do any lines that you have marked with a cross.

Finding Your Hexagrams

Now that you have drawn your lines, look at the hexagram illustrations and find one that matches yours. For the time being, ignore any crosses that you may have marked. This procedure takes a little time and patience, but it serves to take you, or anyone whom you may be guiding, away from the hustle and bustle of daily life. The procedure puts you into a slightly meditative frame of mind.

Basic Hexagram Reading

If all six lines of your hexagram have been arrived at by throwing two heads and one tail or vice versa, find the hexagram in the following illustrations, look it up in the interpretation section in this book and read it as it is. Ignore the instructions that follow, which refer to specific lines. In this case, the chances are that the question or situation is coming to a conclusion.

The Hexagrams of the I Ching

1   2   3   4

5   6   7   8

9   10   11   12

13   14   15   16

17   18   19   20

21   22   23   24

25   26   27   28

29   30   31   32

The Hexagrams of the I Ching

33	34	35	36
37	38	39	40
41	42	43	44
45	46	47	48
49	50	51	52
53	54	55	56
57	58	59	60
61	62	63	64

If you have one or more lines that are marked with a cross, this suggests that the situation is likely to continue for some time to come. The I Ching will then show you whether this is something that you have to learn to live with or whether you can improve it, abandon it, or change it for the better in some way. In the case of a hexagram that contains one or more changing lines, you have several steps to take. The first three are simple.

~ Find the matching hexagram in the illustration and locate it in the interpretation chapter in this book.
~ Read the interpretation for the hexagram.
~ Read the interpretation for the line or lines that are marked with a cross.

Now swap over any marked lines. Thus, a yang line becomes a yin one and vice versa. This will give you a new hexagram. Mark the changed line or lines with a cross and repeat the process.

Some I Ching experts assert that you should not bother to read the changing lines on your second hexagram, because the hexagram itself represents the end of the matter, but I leave this up to you.

The Trigrams

This is where the I Ching gets really interesting. At this point, you can pull your hexagrams apart to make two trigrams. As always with the I Ching, you must start with the bottom line and work upwards. Draw the lower three lines on a piece of paper and mark this "inner trigram." Then draw the upper three lines and mark this "outer trigram."

Lower / Inner Trigram   **Upper / Outer Trigram**

Hexagram

There are eight possible trigram patterns, and each contains many correspondences, just as the signs of the zodiac do in Western astrology. One of the more useful links relates to family members and other people who are traditionally associated with the trigrams. A little thought and imagination will help you make the connection to those who have some influence on your life and who have a bearing on the reading.

The trigrams also refer to body parts—and these might be important to someone who is sick. I have also included the colors that correspond with the trigrams because these can be important—for example, when you are considering the kind of outfit that you need for a specific occasion, or a logo, a trademark, or the color on a letterhead. The color of someone's front door might be significant to you, or it might help you choose the right house to live in. Directions may be handy when you have to choose between something that takes you to the northeast, the south, and so forth. A number may be significant, as might the energy that is represented by the trigram. These concepts need a bit of thought, but they will become clearer when you look at your question and the circumstances that surround it.

One concept that I have deliberately left out is that of the elements (wood, fire, earth, metal, water). A person who knows Chinese astrology will make an immediate connection to the kind of person or situation in the reading by the presence of a particular element (i.e. metal = determined, unyielding, and obstinate). A Westerner who is not into Chinese astrology would not know about this.

Now consider the lower trigram as the inner part of the equation. This means considering *your* point of view, what *you* want, and the way that *your* actions might impinge on the situation or upon others. See the upper trigram as the outer part of the equation, which represents what *other* people want, *their* opinions, *their* actions, and so on. The outer trigram may also refer to situations that are beyond our control—such as bad weather, a strike, a tree falling across the road just when you need to drive down it, or something similar.

A particular family member (father, mother, sister) might be involved in your reading. The same goes for a person you look upon as a parent figure, brother or sister figure, and so on. There may be a direction that is important to you or to someone else who is involved in your life. The time of the year or even the time of day may be significant. The nature of the trigrams may throw a great deal of extra light on your reading, so use these in addition to the hexagrams and their changing lines when contemplating your situation in depth.

Note: I have included the planets in the list of correspondences because many Western astrologers are familiar with their meanings and energies. For example, when faced with two trigrams, the two planets should be considered to be in conjunction, and the nature of the conjunction depends upon the two planets that are involved.

A Brief Review

Read your hexagram as a whole.

If you have marked any lines with a cross, read these.

Split your hexagram into two trigrams. These trigrams may indicate something that bears on your question, such as day, night, north, south, red, blue, a body part, or something else.

Read the trigram that is formed by the lower three lines first. This signifies the things that you want or that are going on in your mind.

Read the trigram formed by the upper three lines of the hexagram. This trigram suggests outside influences that may bear on your question.

Now take the lines that you have marked with a cross and swap them over so that any yang lines are now yin and vice versa. This makes a second hexagram.

Read the new hexagram, its crossed line (or lines) and the trigrams that it makes.

The Trigrams in Detail

The concept of the trigrams is subtle due to their tendency to link together to form hexagrams. If you were to split one trigram off and put it with another, the picture would change. (Remember, I Ching means "Book of Changes.") The trigrams are seen as dynamic, reflecting the fact that nothing in life stays the same forever.

There are eight opportunities for both the upper and lower trigrams to be the same shape, while all other hexagrams are formed by a combination of two different trigrams. When a hexagram is formed by a double trigram (i.e. the same pattern above as below), the meaning of the hexagram is intensified and it suggests that you need to pay extra heed to the guidance given or the situation that is depicted.

The Eight Trigrams

Rather like our Western zodiac, which starts with Aries and ends with Pisces, the trigrams are always listed in the following order and with the attributes shown:

≡≡≡

1 Ch'ien

Name:	Heaven
Family member:	Father
Body parts:	Head, mind and cranium
Season:	Late autumn
Direction:	Northwest
Nature:	Strong, creative, movement
Planet:	Heaven
Time:	Daytime
Motion:	Upward
Color:	White, gold
Number:	Six

Qualities and Associations

Masculine, strong, clever, brave, active, solid, decisive, vital, moving, powerful, untiring strength, takes the initiative, Heaven, God, male, light-giving, virtuous, good, the father, a prince, roundness, cold, ice, the leader or ruler, direct, aggressive, forceful, rigid, unyielding, firm, a time to be strong.

This pure yang trigram is one of the two most powerful of all the trigrams. It is entirely masculine and it represents action, drive, and energy. *Ch'ien* represents the power of heaven or the power that is held by the head of a family or organization. It represents authority, power, strength, creativity, logic, and courage. *Ch'ien* suggests a time when you must focus your mind and energies on a particular goal in order to achieve your ambition. This can be a matter related to your career, studying for an exam, writing a book, looking for love, or achieving any goal that you have in mind. *Ch'ien* shows a desire to be in control and to put things in order.

2 K'un

Name:	Earth
Family member:	Mother (also stands for the ordinary person or a member of the public)
Body parts:	Stomach, abdomen, and womb
Season:	Late summer
Direction:	Southwest
Nature:	Patient, devoted, docile, submissive
Planet:	Earth
Time:	Night
Motion:	Downward
Color:	Black, dark colors
Number:	Two

Qualities and Associations

Feminine, receptive, passive, weak, responsive, yielding, devoted, flexible, soft, calm, wife, patient, moderate, empty, cowardly, maternal, docile, capacious, submissive, subordinate, compliant, obscure, sustaining power, gentle, building.

This entirely feminine trigram is the second of the two most important trigrams. The three broken lines of *K'un* symbolize earth as a support for human life as well as the burial ground for death. The earth is soft and receptive and it can take punishment with a high degree of tolerance. *K'un* seeks to leave things as they are. Loyalty and practicality combine with inner strength, so that a *K'un* person is one who you can turn to in a crisis. *K'un* represents the attributes of care, nurturing, and consideration for others. It relates to feelings and emotions as well as intuition. The key ideas associated with *K'un* are receptivity, endurance, acceptance, patience, and docility.

☳

3 Chen

Name:	Thunder
Family member:	Eldest son (or a strong worker, leader, artist, or inventor)
Body parts:	Foot, throat and voice
Season:	Spring
Direction:	East
Nature:	Arousing, strong, mobile, exciting, power
Planet:	Mars
Motion:	Upward
Color:	Yellow
Trees:	Evergreens, blossoms, bamboo
Number:	Three

Qualities and Associations

Movement, initiative, active, excited, diligent, angry, nervous, threatening, anxious, successful, flying, shocking, motion, growth, vehemence, forceful, decision, development.

The two broken lines on top convey the image of a lightning strike and the bottom solid line symbolizes elevation. Thus, the image is that of lighting striking the top of a mountain. *Chen* symbolizes the birth of an idea and the independence and assertion to act on it. Shock tactics can be used to gain effect and can produce revolutionary results. *Chen* is associated with regeneration. It represents male arousal and sexuality, fertility, initiative, action, and energy.

$$\overline{\overline{}}\ \ \overline{\overline{}}$$

4 K'an

Name:	Water
Family member:	Middle son (also aggressive or difficult young men)
Body parts:	Ear, kidneys
Season:	Winter
Direction:	North
Nature:	Dangerous, cunning, difficult
Planet:	Moon
Motion:	Downward
Color:	Blue
Number:	One

Qualities and Associations

Enveloping, deceitful, aimless, clever, wise, sad, harmless, melancholy, depressed, rain, disturbing, hidden, concealed, blood, fear, moon, dark, work, a pit as in a deep hole, the abyss, hidden things, anxiety, thieves.

A solid line between two broken lines symbolizes water. The two broken lines represent riverbanks with a river running between them. The solid line in the middle represents motion, and creates the image of a fast-flowing river. *K'an* is individualistic and self reliant, believing in doing things for itself. The masculine line in the midst of two feminine lines represents a form of transition or changes that can bring danger.

K'an represents turning points or times when one is not in control of events. Uncertainty, unpredictable times, danger, and stress are shown by this trigram. In favorable circumstances, the change can be a challenge; at other times it is something to be feared. It shows hard times, and that your desires are unlikely to be fulfilled for the time being.

≡≡ ≡≡

5 Ken

Name:	Mountain
Family member:	Youngest son (or priests, monks, prisoners, hospitalized people, and boys younger than sixteen)
Body parts:	Hand, spine
Season:	Early spring
Direction:	Northeast
Nature:	Still, quiet, arresting, immovable
Metal:	Lead
Planet:	Saturn
Motion:	Downward
Color:	Violet
Number:	Eight

Qualities and Associations

Unmoving, calm, gate or door, pausing, inner reserve, keeping still, stopping, quiet, independent, hard, obstinate, perverse, stubborn, slow, indecisive, tough, secretive, contradictory, resting.

A solid line above two broken lines symbolizes a mountain. The solid line represents height, and the bottom two broken lines represent earth as a base, thus this image is a mountain elevated above the earth. It represents keeping still and holding onto the past to keep things as they were. *Ken* represents a time of retreat and reflection when spiritual issues take precedence over worldly ones. Earthly concerns can be forgotten while one concentrates on religious or philosophical ideas. It shows a time of silence, isolation, and withdrawal. Those represented by this trigram seek seclusion, or they may find themselves temporarily secluded, hospitalized, or otherwise cut off from life.

6 Sun

Name:	Wind or wood
Family member:	Eldest daughter (women up to middle age, travelers, businesspeople)
Body parts:	Thigh, upper arm, lungs, and nerves
Season:	Early summer
Direction:	Southeast
Nature:	Gentle, adaptable, flexible
Metal:	Copper
Planet:	Venus
Motion:	Downward
Color:	Green
Number:	Four

Qualities and Associations

Penetrating, indecisive, weak, fragrant, neat, obedient, restless, excitable, bland, mild, and in pursuit of gain.

Two solid lines above a broken line symbolize wind. The two solid lines represent the sky while the broken line represents earth. The wind is invisible, and we can see its existence only by observing the moving treetops. *Sun* represents evolution, slow growth, and gradual change for the better. It represents feminine virtues of endurance, gentle determination, adaptability, and fair play.

≡≡ ≡≡

	7 Li
Name:	Fire
Family member:	Middle daughter (or young women, craftsmen, and artists)
Body parts:	Eyes, blood, and heart
Season:	Summer
Direction:	South
Nature:	Clinging, beautiful, intelligent, light, reason, clarity
Metal:	Mercury
Planet:	Mercury
Motion:	Upward
Color:	Orange
Number:	Nine

Qualities and Associations

Flight, bird, flame, weapons, the sun, brightness, elegance, light-giving, hot, agitated, brilliance, dependable, dedicated, enlightened, dry.

A broken line between two solid lines symbolizes fire. The two solid lines show the movement of a fire. The broken line is the still center of the fire. *Li* represents mutual support, welfare, helping others, illumination, inspiration, clarity, and knowledge. It represents those who are generous and big hearted.

$$\equiv\!\equiv$$

8 T'ui

Name:	Marsh or lake
Family member:	Youngest daughter (or girls up to
the age of	sixteen, mistresses)
Body parts:	Mouth, lips, and tongue
Season:	Autumn
Direction:	West
Nature:	Joyful, sensual
Planet:	Jupiter
Motion:	Upward
Color:	Red
Number:	Seven

Qualities and Associations

Reservoir, gaiety, pleasure, to break into pieces or break apart, mist, attraction, complacent, happy, gossipy, slanderous, laughing, smiling, critical, quarrelsome, contentment, sorcery, tranquility.

A broken line on top of two solid lines symbolizes a marsh. The top broken line is water and the solid lines symbolize the sky. If we look down at a body of water, we see the sky reflected in it. *T'ui* is inventive, entrepreneurial, and always ready to do business. It represents the psychic world, and it is also associated with healing, magic, joy, and pleasure. *T'ui* often refers to women who have no power within the family—such as mistresses or friends.

Quick Fix Interpretations

The I Ching is designed to be slow, meditative, and contemplative. This is enjoyable when you have time to spare, but for occasions when you need a quick answer, here are interpretations to point you in the right direction.

Throw your coins and create your six lines, starting with the bottom one and working upward. Look up your hexagram in the key and read the answer in this chapter. Do not bother with lines, trigrams, or hidden meanings—just read the quick-fix interpretations.

1. Ch'ien. Creativity. The King.

Persist and create, make your efforts last. Success is indicated. Decisive action brings good fortune. Be creative and do what is right.

2. K'un. Receptivity. The Queen.

Take time to nourish the things that are in your life and to bring things into being. Perseverance helps you to succeed.

3. Chun. Difficulty at the beginning.

Finding the right location or the right kind of living and working space is the key to success. This will be a time of growth and release from tension.

4. Meng. Youth, folly, inexperience.

Do not act yet, because you are not ready. A lack of experience will land you in hot water if you act rashly.

5. Hsu. Waiting.

Wait for the time to become right for action. Eating and drinking with others will be pleasant or important in some way.

6. Sung. Conflict.

Take advice from people who have more experience. Avoid arguments and conflict and if necessary, avoid (or be prepared for) lawsuits.

7. Shih. Leadership.

Show leadership and respect to those who rely on you, and use your authority to ensure their obedience. You may be experiencing inner conflict of some kind.

8. Pi. Joining.

Change the people with whom you associate, and change the way in which you put things together. The timing of relationships is important now.

9. Hsiao Ch'u. Restraint, gathering small things.

Accumulate small things that can be put together to make something great. This is a beneficial time for anything related to the raising of children.

10. Lu. Treading.

Find your way one step at a time, and trust in the outcome. Pleasant manners lead toward success.

11. T'ai. Harmony.

Success is linked to tranquility. Be peaceful and flexible, but be true to yourself. You will be protected by the spiritual connection between heaven and earth.

12. P'i. Stagnation.

Beware of pride without substance. Do not get carried away with anything.

13. T'ung jen. Community.

All will be well if you act with honesty and flexibility. Cooperate and be steadfast. Harmonious relationships are indicated.

14. Ta yu. Wealth.

This is the time to be great. Concentrate, produce things, and share the results with others. Concentrate your mental and physical energy and use both now.

15. Ch'ien. Modesty.

Think and speak humbly in order to accomplish your goals. Heaven rewards the humble now.

16. Yu. Enthusiasm.

Prepare now for enjoyment later. Happiness and enthusiasm will carry you through.

17. Sui. Following.

Go with the flow. To lead, you must also know how to serve.

18. Ku. Decay.

Find the source of the corruption. This hexagram actually warns about danger from putrefaction and poison, especially that of venomous insects. (You may need to read this one figuratively rather than literally. If cleanliness or insects are a problem, use some diluted bleach or an antibacterial cleaner in the kitchen, bathroom, and elsewhere, and squirt some insecticide around the place!)

19. Lin. Gathering strength.
Welcome what is approaching, because good fortune is on the way.

20. Kuan. Contemplating.
Let things come into view and then work out what is going on. Take a class, contemplate, and meditate.

21. Shih Ho. Biting through.
Stress the positive achievements that you have made, and do not allow others to stress the negative. Interference in your marriage or relationship will soon pass away.

22. Pi. Grace, adorning.
Beautify things and be brave. Beauty, adornment, and embellishment are important in some way, so this might be a good time to spend some money on your appearance.

23. Po. Instability.
Strip away old ideas and habits. Cut or prune things down to the essentials.

24. Fu. Turning point.
Go back and welcome a new beginning. A change of seasons will bring a renewal of energy.

25. Wu Wang. Innocence.
Disentangle yourself from difficulties, and trust your intuition. A childlike innocence will help you more than trying to be clever.

26. Ta ch'u. Great accumulating.

Concentrate, focus, and be active. Abundance is symbolized by the raising of pasture animals. (Animals were considered to be a source of wealth in olden times, and for those who farm them they still are, so this one can be read figuratively or literally depending upon your lifestyle.)

27. I. Nourishment.

Accept what has already happened. Nourish and encourage others, and consider your loved ones. Take some rest.

28. Ta Kuo. Great excess.

Gather your forces, and do not be afraid to act alone. This hexagram is linked with new growth.

29. K'an. Water, a ravine, danger.

Collect your forces and take a risk. Be careful, because you are in danger of being trapped.

30. Li. Clinging fire.

Think logically and take an intellectual approach. Spread light and warmth among others.

31. Hsien. Relating, attraction.

This may mark the start of a love affair or a successful working partnership. This is a time of unity and cooperation.

32. Heng. Persevering.

Carry on and renew your efforts. Do not insist on having things your own way.

33. Tun. Retreat.

Retreat and be happy staying in the background. This is not a good time for speculation or for business, so step back for a while.

34. Ta Chuang. Great power.

Have a firm sense of purpose and go forward. Focus your mind and your energies and take the initiative.

35. Chin. Progress.

Be ready to give and receive. Your fortunes are improving, but you must avoid aggression.

36. Ming I. Darkening of the light.

Hide your light for a while and accept difficulties. Be cautious and restrained but do not allow misery to grind you down.

37. Chia Jen. Family.

Stay with your loved ones. Households and family life are what will count now.

38. K'ui. Opposition.

Be aware of what is going on. Turn conflict into creative tension. Do not insist that you are right—allow others to have their own opinions.

39. Chien. Obstruction.

Rethink the situation. This is a poor time for everything, especially love relationships.

40. Hsieh. Liberation.

Solve your problems by untying the knots that bind you. If something or someone is weighing you down or if the situation is no longer working, let it go.

41. Sun. Decrease.

Mist below mountains means that you cannot see where you are going. If you are doing too much or if you are involved in too many things, let something go.

42. I. Increase.

Expand what you do during this fertile time. Abundance and wealth are in store for you.

43. Kuai. Determination.

Make a decision and act with resolution. The outlook for money and business is good, but it would be worth taking out insurance.

44. Kou. Encountering, temptation.

Welcome what is happening but be prepared to let go if necessary. The union of male and female is auspicious.

45. Ts'ui. Gathering.

A great effort brings great rewards. You will soon meet someone who will be important to you.

46. Sheng. Advancing.

Make an effort and move forward step by step. If you have done the groundwork, the project will take off.

47. K'un. Oppression.

Look within yourself to find the way to break free. Adverse times build character, so do not run away from trouble.

48. Ching. The well.

Communicate and network with others. If you need to make tough choices, pray to your gods and use your intuition.

49. Ko. Revolution.

Strip away the old. Shed old ideas like a snake sheds its skin.

50. Ting. The cauldron, holding.

Hold on to and transform your problem. Ensure that your tools, equipment, mode of transport, and so on are in good working order.

51. Chen. Turmoil.

Stormy weather is ahead, but do not panic. You will soon deal with new things that might be hard to cope with for a while, until you get used to them.

52. Ken. Stillness.

Keep calm. Do not take unnecessary gambles or take on more work than you can handle. Peace and love can be expected in the home.

53. Chien. Gradual advance.

Go slowly, step by step, and advance like a tortoise. This is a good time for love and marriage.

54. Kuei Mei. The marrying maiden.

If you are being victimized or treated badly, stay put for the time being, because it looks as though things will change of their own accord. Realize your hidden potential.

55. Feng. Abundance.

Prosperity and happiness are around you, but you must not overspend or overexpand. Give, but do not leave yourself short.

56. Lu. Traveling.
You may feel as though you are on the outside of a situation, but you will gain by making inquiries. Traveling and journeys—especially solitary journeys—are fortunate.

57. Sun. Penetrating.
Gently penetrate to the heart of the problem. The energy of trees and plants that can bend with the wind might inspire you.

58. Tui. Joy.
Express yourself and join with others. Family life will soon be good. You will have peace of mind.

59. Huan. Dispersing.
A change of location is on the way, and you may leave loved ones or colleagues behind for a while. Clear away whatever is blocking you or clouding the light.

60. Chieh. Limitation.
Teamwork and going by other people's rules will help you now. Keep your opinions to yourself. When the time is right, you will be able to take charge of the situation once again.

61. Chung Fu. Inner truth.
Be true to yourself and others and you will gain their trust. Connect your inner life with your outer life. Career, business, money, and love are all looking good now. A change of residence is possible.

62. Ksiao Kuo. Moderation.
Progress will be halted, but do not allow worry or negativity to get you down. Carefully adapt to each of the situations that surround you.

63. Chi Chi. Completion.

A cycle has already ended, and the situation is already changing. Do not act yet; allow things to settle down. Guard against losing what you have gained. Marriage and love are successful at this time.

64. Wei Chi. Before completion.

The previous hexagram is called completion, but this one means before completion. This suggests that you need to tie up loose ends before moving on to something new, so gather your energy for a decisive new move.

In a way, these two hexagrams are a little like the last two cards in the Major Arcana of the Tarot. In the Tarot, the second-to-last card is Judgment, which represents judgment day, the last trumpet, and so on, but this is followed by the World card, which signifies the end of a cycle and tying up loose ends in anticipation of the start of a new one.

Timing and the I Ching

The answers in the hexagrams do not usually contain specific information about the timescale of the events or opportunities they describe. They look at the past, present, or future in general and the inner world as well as the outer—and they offer advice and understanding. Some of the original texts carry references to three days or three years; however, these timings are not to be taken literally. To the ancient Chinese, three was a general term for "several," so three days meant a pause for thought and three years meant a long time. Additionally, seven days meant a naturally completed period of time. Although it may be useful to examine the inner time of your experience and to see whether you will change or whether your attitudes and activities will change in time, this does not help when you are looking at the calendar!

When you have done the reading for the first hexagram, take note of any moving lines, then swap the yang lines for yin ones and vice versa to reach your second hexagram. The first hexagram describes your current situation and what is unfolding in the near future. The second hexagram describes how things will develop in the more distant future.

Now, take your first hexagram and look at all the lines in the list rather than just those that change. The bottom line will assess the beginning of the situation or something that has recently passed. The top line refers to a later time and to events that still lie in the future. Only the four middle lines represent the time that is active within the situation. The respective positions of the lines show the sequence of events, reading from the bottom upwards. The lines that you have marked with a cross show the precise points of change.

Now take your second hexagram and read the lines from bottom to top. All the events depicted will be in the future—starting with the near future and working forward to the distant future.

Timing on the Trigrams

Each of the trigrams refers to a specific time of year, so it is easy to see how a certain season might be relevant to your question.

1. Ch'ien: Late fall

2. K'un: Late summer

3. Chen: Spring

4. K'an: Winter

5. Ken: Early spring

6. Sun: Early summer

7. Li: Summer

8. Tui: Fall

The trigrams also relate to specific times of day and to certain periods of time. As usual, the first two trigrams (*Ch'ien*, heaven and *K'un*, earth) are the most important.

1. Ch'ien: Daytime. Just before midnight. A period of one day or one day into the future.

2. K'un: Night. Afternoon. A period of one month or one month into the future.

3. Chen: Early morning.

4. K'an: Midnight.

5. Ken: Just before dawn.

6. Sun: Mid-morning.

7. Li: Noon.

8. Tui: Evening or late afternoon.

The I Ching in More Detail

Some people enjoy details and playing around with possibilities, but others do not. If you appreciate data, the following will give you something to think about. This chapter contains some intriguing ways of looking more deeply into your readings.

Yin and Yang

Yin and yang are mutually dependent opposites. Looking at the world in terms of yin and yang gives one a real sense of how dynamic and ever-changing the universe is. In addition, no matter how you are feeling today, things are bound to change. As the Chinese say, you can never step into the same river twice. This is because the river may look the same, but the water that you stepped into the first time will have moved downstream when you try to step into it again.

Yin originally meant "shady, secret, dark, mysterious, and cold." It could mean the shaded north side of a mountain. Yang meant "clear, bright, the sun, and heat," and thus the lighted south side of a mountain. From these basic opposites, a complete system developed. Yin represents everything about the world that is dark, hidden, passive, receptive, yielding, cool, soft, and feminine. Yang represents everything about the world that is illuminated, evident, active, aggressive, controlling, hot, hard, and masculine.

Everything can be identified as either yin or yang. Earth is the ultimate yin object and Heaven is the ultimate yang object. Although yin is feminine and yang masculine, most things (and many people) are a mixture of the two. The familiar circular symbol of yin and yang flowing into each other shows the yin side with a yang dot within it and vice versa. This symbolizes the fact that each force contains the seed of the other and that under certain circumstances, they can actually become the other.

Yin and Yang Characteristics

	Yin	Yang
Nature	Feminine	Masculine
	Passive	Active
	Receives	Creates
	Soft	Hard
	Dark	Bright
Symbols	Moon	Sun
	Tiger	Dragon
	North	South
Color	Black	Red
Numbers	Even	Odd

Chinese character	陰	陽
Original meaning	North side of a hill (away from the sun)	South side of a hill (facing the sun)

The earliest oracles confined themselves to yes or no answers. This is the basis of the I Ching. Yes was indicated by a simple, horizontal unbroken line and No by a broken line. This was obviously far too simplistic, so gradually the single lines were combined in pairs, and then a third line was added. In this way the eight trigrams came into being.

More About Trigrams

Yang and Yin Placements in the Trigrams

Odd numbers are always considered to be yang, while even numbers are always seen as yin. Therefore, lines 1, 3, and 5 below are yang, and lines 2, 4, and 6 are yin. If a yang line is in a yang place or if a yin line in a yin place, they are considered to be well placed. If a yin line is in a yang place, it is unequal to the task at hand. If a yang line is in a yin place, it is too aggressive for the situation.

Corresponding Lines in the Two Trigrams

Split your hexagram into its two trigrams as illustrated below:

Line 6	———
Line 5	—— ——
Line 4	———
Line 3	—— ——
Line 2	—— ——
Line 1	———

Line 3	—— ——
Line 2	—— ——
Line 1	———

Line 6	———
Line 5	—— ——
Line 4	———

When the corresponding lines are the same (both yang or both yin), they are in opposition and are therefore unhelpful to each other. When they are different, they are helpful to one another. In this illustration, the lowest and middle lines oppose each other while the top lines are helpful. This might make two different trigrams less awkward than they would otherwise be.

More About Hexagrams

Complementary Hexagrams

Any hexagram has a mirror image. Draw your hexagram and then draw another one beside it. To do this, swap over each solid line for a broken line and vice versa; then read the interpretation for the second hexagram. This shows the exact *opposite* of what is happening to you. Looking at this hexagram may throw some light on the situation.

The Nuclear Hexagram

In this hexagram, the top and bottom lines are disregarded, and lines 2, 3, and 4 become the lower trigram, while lines 3, 4, and 5 become the upper trigram. The nuclear hexagram shows a hidden possibility at the heart of your situation. This may issue a warning or point out an opportunity that you are not yet aware of. This describes something that might eventually emerge from your situation.

The Hexagram of Sequence

This is the hexagram that immediately precedes the one you have cast. For example, if you cast hexagram No. 27, the previous hexagram in the list will be No. 26. This reveals the root of your situation, or something you have to acknowledge or work on before you can exploit the current situation's full potential.

More About Lines

Development of a Situation

The lowest line of the hexagram depicts the onset of the situation. Line 2 shows the condition beginning to grow stronger. Line 3 is at the top of the lower trigram, so the condition is now unstable, because line 3 is about to leave the lower trigram for the upper trigram. Line 4 denotes that the condition is approaching its maximum potential and therefore suggests caution. Line 5 indicates that the condition has reached its maximum potential. The top line means that the condition depicted has exceeded its maximum potential and that it is changing into something else.

Another Interpretation

Line 1 represents the time shortly before the present problem or question came into being. The middle lines relate to the question as it is now—these are described as active. Line 6 represents the period just after the active time when the problem is solved or when something else starts to take its place.

Too Many Lines?

When you get a hexagram with 3, 4, or 5 moving lines, it can be difficult to make sense of the apparently contradictory information. You can choose to read the lines in sequence, starting with the lowest and moving upwards. However, there are several ways to reduce multiple lines to just one—and this being a Chinese form of divination, there is no shortage of possibilities:

> If there are two moving lines, one yin, and one yang, consult the yin line.
> If there are two moving lines of the same kind, consult the lower one.
> If there are three moving lines, consult the middle one.

If there are four moving lines, consult the upper of the two unmoving lines.

If there are five moving lines, consult the one unmoving line.

If there are six moving lines, just consult the relevant hexagram, except in hexagrams 1 and 2, where you should read all six lines.

If this flummoxes you, let your intuition select one line and read that!

Interpreting the Hexagrams

In this chapter, I give the full description for each hexagram, including the two trigrams that make up the hexagram, notes about the image that is behind the hexagram, the keywords that are associated with each hexagram, and a detailed interpretation. Then I give the interpretations for each of the lines that are associated with each hexagram.

1. Ch'ien. Creativity. The King.
Upper trigram: Ch'ien. Creativity. Heaven.
Lower trigram: Ch'ien. Creativity. Heaven.

The Image
There are two trigrams in every hexagram, and this usually denotes that there is some kind of movement or change of fortune that can occur due to the switching back and forth of energy between the two trigrams. This is one reason why the I Ching is known as The Book of Changes. However, heaven is supremely powerful, it does not get tired, it does not suddenly decide to stop being heaven—and there is only one heaven. The doubling of any trigram indicates movement, but in the case of *Ch'ien*, this is in the sense that time always moves onward, we must impose our ideas and our wills upon it. One revolution of heaven makes a day, and the repetition shows that each day is followed by another. Since heaven is

unchanging, this hexagram can remind us that everything can and does change—eventually.

Keywords

Power, sublime, success, persevering, spirit, creative energy, dynamism, endurance, strength, tenacity, action, inspiration, clearing away, great, originating, penetrating, advantageous, correct, and firm.

Interpretation

Made up from two *Ch'ien* trigrams, *Ch'ien* is pure yang and the most masculine, fatherly, and muscular of the hexagrams. Determination will be needed in order to change and transform a situation. To get what you want, you need to act bravely and confidently. Although obstacles lie ahead, persistence will overcome them. Focus on your goals and go all out for what you want. Initiate new ideas and use your energy wisely. At work, you need to show leadership and strength. In your personal life, your loved ones will turn to you for direction. It is important to use your strength wisely without being aggressive or obstinate. This could be the beginning of a new phase in your life.

Ch'ien represents the start of something that is advantageous, correct, and firm. It shows benevolence, righteousness, propriety, and knowledge. Success will come, and everything depends upon your actively seeking happiness and persevering with what you know to be right. You can bring peace and security through creating order.

The Lines

Lowest line

Do not act yet. Your talents have not been recognized. Remain true to yourself and wait because the time is not yet right.

Second line up
Your ability to bring matters to the forefront is growing. Let your ideas flow and settle into shape. Your seriousness, reliability, and influence make you look good in the eyes of others. Contact those who can help you.

Third line up
All day you are busy and all night your mind is in turmoil. Your creative energy is on the increase. There is much to be done, so when others rest, you worry. It is time to turn your back on the past, even though what you did in the past was right. Your influence is growing.

Fourth line up
This is a period of transition. You need to choose between soaring to the heights and playing an important part in the world or withdrawing into solitude to develop yourself. So long as you are true to yourself you will find the best way.

Fifth line up
Seek out people who can help you. Make things, build, create, and establish. Your influence is increasing.

Top line
Avoid arrogance. You will regret it if you try to enforce your authority. If you go overboard you will have cause for regret. Pride leads to a fall.

When all the lines are marked for change, it means that the whole hexagram is in motion and it will change into the hexagram *K'un*, which means passivity and receptivity rather than action.

2. K'un. Receptivity. The Queen.

Upper trigram: K'un. Receptivity. Earth.
Lower trigram: K'un. Receptivity. Earth.

The Image

As is the case with heaven, the earth is unchanging, so the doubling of the trigram means that the usual change and movement that occurs when the energies switch back and forth between the trigrams is absent. The earth will never change much—whatever good or harm is done to it. The figure, which is made up of six divided lines, expresses the ideal of subordination and docility. It represents nature in contrast to spirit, earth in contrast to heaven, and the maternal female rather than the paternal male. There is only one earth, so the doubled trigram implies endurance.

Keywords

The visible world, power to give things form, mother, servant, receptive power, welcome, consent, yielding, giving birth, nourishing, originating, penetrating, providing, serving, working for and working with.

Interpretation

Made up from two *K'un* trigrams, *K'un* is pure yin, the most feminine and motherly of the hexagrams. This suggests that you may need to adjust to circumstances, fit in, and not make waves. You are confronted with many conflicting forces. To some extent your future happiness is in the hands of others or else it involves others—so it is important to not just think of yourself. However, you still need to maintain your sense of purpose and do what needs to be done. Trying to take the lead can make you go astray—you need guidance at this time.

The feminine virtues of endurance, duty, fitting in, and waiting for things to turn out right are emphasized. You have the power to accept the inevitable. Although times can be confusing, do not worry. You need to go with the flow for a while and trust your intuition. Joining others for concrete purposes will achieve a lot. By yielding and providing what is needed, you can open up a new cycle. Accept that some things are hidden from you, and do not set up boundaries about what you will or will not do.

The Lines

Lowest line
Act carefully, establish a base. Things begin to solidify.

Second line up
Focus on a single idea. Establish that first, and as long as you are sincere, you will be able to achieve this one aim. Do not try to take on any more than you already have on your plate, and do not take on anything new, because you have not yet worked out all that needs to be done.

Third line up
You should not bring your part in things to an end because you and your efforts need to be visible. You can be successful on behalf of others. Send out feelers in new directions, and you will make important discoveries.

Fourth line up
What you want is out there waiting for you. Whatever you do will be acceptable, so you will neither be blamed nor praised for your efforts. Think before you act.

Fifth line up
Sticking to what works, avoiding foolish ideas, and acting with discretion will bring supreme good fortune.

Top line
Do not let a situation of conflict continue. If you are responsible for the impasse, give in to restore the peace.

When all the lines are marked for change, it is time to take action rather than sitting things out.

3. Chun. Difficulty at the beginning.

Upper trigram: K'an. The abyss. Water.
Lower trigram: Chen. The arousing. Thunder.

The Image

The image associated with *Chun* is that of a blade of grass, struggling to grow from the earth and gradually rising above the surface. These first stages of growth symbolize the struggle that marks the emergence out of disorder, so this is a time when great changes are made. It brings order out of confusion.

Keywords

Growth, assembling, establishing a base, teething troubles, gathering energy, new possibilities.

Interpretation

This is the start of a new phase, and you do not yet know where it will lead. You do not know the risks you face. You need to strip away old ideas, because everything is changing and you must break new ground now. Although things may get off to a slow start, they will improve. You can reach your goals in a slow and steady manner. You have a lot of work to do. Things come at you from all sides but you can find the help that you will need in order to deal with them. Do not act prematurely or alone. You need helpers, but you should not just leave them to their own devices—lend a hand where it is needed. There is a chance of a new relationship. You will make progress by doing what is right and by persisting. Changes should not be lightly made.

The Lines

Lowest line

You need to establish firm foundations and to take advantage of any help that is offered.

Second line up
Your difficulties pile up. Every time you start something you run into obstacles. You need to make alliances and realize that forces beyond your control are at work.

Third line up
If you continue to act in this way you will lose your direction. Do not reject help when it is offered. Be prepared to give up if the situation demands it and avoid doing something you may regret.

Fourth line up
You need to actively seek alliances because this will help.

Fifth line up
Give people what they need and do not impose your ideas on them.

Top line
Why allow this bad situation to continue? It is time to retreat.

When all the lines can change it means that you must persevere. Stick to your guns and do what is right because then you will benefit.

4. Meng. Youth, folly, inexperience.
Upper trigram: Ken. Keeping still. Mountain.
Lower trigram: Kan. The abyss. Water.

The Image
The image is of a spring welling up at the foot of the mountain and it is considered to be an image of youth. The water flows out but it does not yet know what direction to take. *Meng* suggests youthful inexperience and ignorance.

Keywords

Cover, hide conceal, unaware, ignorant, uneducated, young, undeveloped, unseen beginnings, nurture inner growth.

Interpretation

You are immature and you may have a clouded view of your problem because you do not really know what you are doing. You need to gain or update your skills or obtain an education or qualifications. Take advice and learn slowly. Sometimes you feel confused and need to work through things steadily until you understand them. If you are misunderstood, take the time to explain yourself to others. You may have a one-sided view of things. Do not put on airs and graces but be ready to listen to advice. Treat others kindly and generously. There is nothing wrong with being inexperienced. Seek out someone wiser and more experienced than yourself to offer you the advice that you need.

The Lines

Lowest line
Restrain those who do things wrongly—but do not keep an unnecessarily tight control on yourself. However, you will need to be self-disciplined to avoid making a fool of yourself.

Second line up
You need to take a responsible attitude and to care for things. Be kind to those who know less than you do.

Third line up
Do not be grasping. It does you no good to rely on status symbols or material things, even though you feel that these will give you satisfaction.

Fourth line up
Your isolation distances you from what is real, so you need to correct your thinking. Acting in ignorance will give you cause for regret.

Fifth line up

You get what you want by yielding and by gently working toward your goal. Although you are inexperienced, things turn out well.

Top line

You need to resist the temptation to break the rules or behave violently. Work within your situation rather than fighting it.

5. Hsu. Waiting.

Upper trigram: K'an. The abyss. Water.
Lower trigram: Ch'ien. Creativity. Heaven.

The Image

This is the image of clouds rising to the heavens. We all need nourishment from above, but it comes in its own time and we may have to wait. The clouds bring rain to refresh all that grows. The rain will come in its own time. We cannot make it come; we have to wait for it.

Keywords

Take care of, serve, look out for, provide what is needed, hesitation, focus, and patience.

Interpretation

By acting sincerely and waiting for the right moment, you can have the success that you want, but you must first find out what is required. You will not hang around unnecessarily right now because you are certain to reach your goal. You are faced with a problem that needs to be overcome. Weakness and impatience can do nothing. It is only when you have the courage to face things exactly as they are, without self-deception or illusion, that the path to success may be recognized. It is up to you to act on that recognition. Although you may feel that you should act boldly and confront what is wrong in your life, it would be better to wait until you are sure of success. You are not in full control of what is happening. There is danger ahead, so do not plunge into anything. If life is quiet, take a rest and wait for busier times to come. Talk over your ideas with others and listen to their advice. Ambition and advancement are on the way, even if they are not evident yet. This is a time to spread harmony and to do the right thing. Others will admire your accomplishments. Crossing water for business or personal reasons can be beneficial.

The Lines

Lowest line

You need to wait in the background. This may be difficult, but perseverance will bring you insight. Maintaining things as they are now will prevent problems in the future.

Second line up

You need to adapt your thoughts to those beneath you and to the ideas that others have. Although you may be the victim of gossip, things will turn out well in the end.

Third line up

You feel bogged down and are unwilling to move if you are to avoid being hurt. You need to understand how you got into this situation and find a way out of it.

Fourth line up

Although you feel stuck in a disastrous place, you can be saved if you are prepared to listen.

Fifth line up

You need to spend time with others and to eat and drink with them. Be reliable, do what is right, and everything will turn out well.

Top line

Three people unexpectedly offer you help that you have not asked for. If you offer them your respect, they will help you out of your present situation.

6. Sung. Conflict.

Upper trigram: Ch'ien. Creativity. Heaven.
Lower trigram: K'an. The abyss. Water.

The Image

Heaven and the abyss are pulling you in two opposing directions. Your life is full of contradiction at present.

Keywords

Argue, dispute, plead, complain, wrangle, controversy, resolve conflicts.

Interpretation

Although you are probably in the right, this is not a good time to argue or make your point. Try to express yourself without escalating a conflict. It does not matter how sincere you are; others will argue with you, and you may have to meet your opponent halfway. Do not be intimidated, but avoid petty arguments because there is a good chance you will lose them. Accept criticism or lack of credit for what you have done for now. Do not attempt large undertakings at work or elsewhere—maintaining a steady course is the best option. It is not a good time to try to complete things. Asking for advice is wise. Act cautiously. Relationships are not favorable at the moment, as this is not a harmonious time.

The Lines

Lowest line
Get out of this affair. Say what you need to say and go. This will avoid a long and bitter conflict.

Second line up
Do not try to control the situation by arguing. It is best to give way and return to where doors are open for you.

Third line up
Take advantage of the work done by your predecessors. You will accomplish what you have been asked to do but you may not receive credit for it.

Fourth line up
Turn away rather than argue. Submit to fate, and an opportunity will come to you.

Fifth line up
State your case confidently and expect good results. You can correct what has gone wrong.

Top line
You may be showered with money and credit, but by the end of the morning you will lose it three times over. This temporary success will gain you nothing in the end.

7. Shih. Leadership.
Upper trigram: K'un. Receptivity. Earth.
Lower trigram: K'an. The abyss. Water.

The Image
The image is of people grouped around a center. It symbolizes water that is stored up in the earth in the same way that strength is stored up in groups of people. This strength is invisible in times of peace but always ready for use as a source of power in times of conflict.

Keywords
Army, collective force, leadership, organize, discipline.

Interpretation
A battle is ahead, and you will need to maintain the confidence of those who depend on you. You are willing and able to take risks and to confront obstacles. Others are close at hand to help you and offer spiritual guidance. Your situation is confusing and it will require care before it is resolved. You

have to decide whether to fight against injustice or retreat. Avoid simply imposing your will on others because you have the capacity to lead, although you still need to develop leadership skills. It takes a lot of strength to capture the hearts of people and to awaken their enthusiasm. Use those whom you respect as role models. The idea is not to fight, but to bring order to a situation and to protect others. Something significant will return to your life if you are open to it. Be firm and act righteously. War is a dangerous thing, so it should only be used only as a last resort.

The Lines

Lowest line

Don't let the rules get in the way of what needs to happen, but ensure that you don't lose sight of the right way of doing things.

Second line up

Three events will show you that those above you will help you to change your life for the better.

Third line up

Rid yourself of old and useless ideas, because hanging on to old baggage will bring misfortune.

Fourth line up

You have not made a mistake. Sometimes retreating is the right move to make.

Fifth line up

Be careful about what you say and do not try to get others to do your work.

Top line

Act on your ideas rather than adapting to those of others. You can achieve something significant at this time.

8. Pi. Joining.

Upper trigram: K'an. The abyss. Water.
Lower trigram: K'un. Receptivity. Earth.

The Image

The image of water and earth together signifies combining things of a different nature. The waters on the surface of the earth flow together wherever they can. This hexagram symbolizes those things that hold together and the laws of physics that make this so. The same idea is suggested by the fact that all the lines of the hexagram except the fifth are yielding. They hold together because they are influenced by a leader who is at their center.

Keywords

Join, ally, find a new center, order things, harmonize, work together and work towards.

Interpretation

Honesty and sincerity will lead to success as long as you cooperate. Unite with others so you can complement and aid each other, and you will discover the place where you belong. Dishonesty will lead to misfortune. You may need to pull together in your job or family and work for the good of those around you as well as for yourself. Get to the heart of the matter. A leader is required to hold things together. You should take on this role only if you are equal to the task. If you are not, then you can only make things worse. There will be a role for you whether or not you are at the center of things. Problems seem to come at you from all sides and you need to be organized. Relationships may dissolve as you discover new ways of putting things together. A new relationship with someone is possible.

The Lines

Lowest line

Have confidence in your group, and be sincere when establishing any relationship.

Second line up

Do not let connections slip away, but make sure that you are with the right group of people. Guard against getting in with the wrong crowd.

Third line up

You are mixing with the wrong people. Be careful that you do not get hurt. There is no need to become intimate with everyone you meet.

Fourth line up

You are outside the group. Test your ideas and stick to your values. You have gained your position by your own efforts and through your own worth.

Fifth line up

Stop being predatory and give way to others at times. Sometimes you need to serve without seeking reward.

Top line

There is no central idea holding this group together, so you should leave before disaster strikes.

9. Hsiao Ch'u. Small accumulating, restraint.

Upper trigram: Sun. Gentleness. Wind.
Lower trigram: Ch'ien. Creativity. Heaven.

The Image

The image reflects the fertile soil of a river delta and the wind blowing across the sky. A weak line in the fourth place holds the five strong lines in check. The wind restrains the clouds but is not strong enough to turn them to rain. A strong element is temporarily kept in check by a weak element, which implies that it is only through gentleness that a successful outcome can be achieved.

Keywords

The taming power of little items, unimportant, adapting to what crosses your path, take in, gather, collect, hoard, control, care for, nurture, support, tame, and raise children.

Interpretation

Conserve your energy and gather whatever you will need for your future plans to be successful. There are obstacles in the way, so you can't do more than make preparations at this time. Be patient and flexible, tolerate what you have to, and do what you can to make those around you comfortable. Times may be hard for a while, but so long as you are sensible you will achieve your aims. Restraint, sincerity, and considerations for the feelings of others are needed. Friendly persuasion will be more successful than sweeping measures. If a relationship is failing, it might be time to leave. Letting go can be an act of love. You need to be determined but also gentle and adaptable.

The Lines

Lowest line

Go back to the start and pursue your own course. Do not use force to get what you want.

Second line up

Something important returns to your life, pulling you back to the past. Hang in there. If your path is blocked, wait for a better time before making a move.

Third line up

Trying to carry such a big load will make you irritable and argumentative. You and your loved ones are trying to avoid true communication.

Fourth line up

Be sincere and try not to be irritable or angry. Avoid conflict. The truth will soon emerge, and that will exert more effect on the situation than the people or things that are creating obstacles.

Fifth line up
You do not have to act alone. Someone around you will offer resources that you can use, and that person will help you.
Top line
Stay where you are for now. If you try to take control of the situation, you will lose your direction.

10. Lu. Treading.
Upper trigram: Ch'ien. Creativity. Heaven.
Lower trigram: Tui. Joy. Lake.

The Image
Heaven above and the lake below symbolize the difference between high and low, so this image refers to the right way to behave. Here the strong tread on the weak, but the weak may make a stand, knowing that it will be accepted with good humor by the strong. The main concern is finding the right way to do things.

Keywords
Walk, step, path, practice, accomplish, conduct, behavior, salary, happiness, luck.

Interpretation
You need to think about how you can make your way in the world. Clarify what you want and what you feel your purpose to be. Leave things until more favorable conditions apply. Be firm, even with yourself, and tread the straight and narrow path. Do not allow others to take advantage of you or force you to lose your stride. When people around you act wildly, remember that pleasant manners succeed even with irritable people. Use your intuition. Although there are difficulties, you can cope with them. Tread gently and plan carefully, then act with humility and caution.

The Lines

Lowest line
Go your own way. You can make progress by using your own inner strength and by keeping things simple.

Second line up
You can smooth things over by continual effort. Stay hidden and work in the background.

Third line up
It is hard to see clearly. You cannot move freely right now, so do not act recklessly.

Fourth line up
Be cautious. By going slowly you will achieve your purpose and overcome danger.

Fifth line up
Leave the old things behind and correct mistakes from the past. You can only be successful by being aware of the dangers ahead.

Top line
You need to examine your behavior and its consequences to judge what you can expect to happen next.

11. T'ai. Harmony.
Upper trigram: K'un. Receptivity. Earth.
Lower trigram: Ch'ien. Creativity. Heaven.

The Image
The influences of heaven and earth meet and are in harmony so that all living things bloom and prosper. This also symbolizes a time of social harmony. The small and weak are about to take their departure, while the great, strong, and good elements are coming on to the scene. This brings good fortune and success.

Keywords
Great, abundant, prosperous, peaceful, fertile, permeate, communicate.

Interpretation
This will be a time of peace, harmony, and joy, so you should share your happiness and good fortune with those who are less well off. You can plant for the future or harvest from the past. There will be good fortune with progress and success. You can now develop your ideas and radically change the group that you associate with. Be firm and adaptable in your dealings. Those above you are willing to help out when needed.

The Lines
Lowest line
Changing the people you associate with and putting things in order will take you forward.

Second line up
You have a problem that only you can sort out and you may need to move away from certain relationships. You will gain credit for your actions.

Third line up
Difficult times come after peaceful times. Let go of something or someone that you care for and if that person or thing returns, you will know where you stand.

Fourth line up
You may need to call on family and friends if you do not have the resources to cope with what is on your plate.

Fifth line up
Joining forces with someone younger helps to gratify your desires and fulfill your aims. Wait for the right moment to act.

Top line
Things feel as if they are collapsing and you need to call on support. This is not a time to test out new ideas.

12. P'i. Stagnation.

Upper trigram: Ch'ien. Creativity. Heaven.
Lower trigram: K'un. Receptivity. Earth.

The Image
Heaven is retreating from you while the earth sinks lower, so this is a time of decline.

Keywords
Closed, stopped, obstacle, unable to advance, deny, refuse, disapprove, bad, evil, unfortunate, unhappy, blocked communication.

Interpretation
Poverty, losses and hard times surround you, but a change in attitude or outlook will help. You have to accept that communications are cut off and that you are being blocked. Do not be discouraged. Good things can emerge from misfortune. Relationships are difficult now, so it is hard for you to know whom to trust or what to do. You are mixing with the wrong people. Be modest, withdraw, and do not make a fuss. Imposing your ideas on others will not work. For the time being, your best bet is to ignore offers that place you in a prominent role and to keep your head down.

The Lines
Lowest line
You need to associate with a different group of people. Follow what you believe in and be prepared to try out your own ideas.
Second line up
Adapt to what crosses your path despite the obstructions that bar your way. You are beginning to understand how to deal with your situation, but this will take time and patience.

Third line up
Do not take on anything heavy; you do not have the confidence or the skills for it yet. Right now, you can hardly cope with your current workload. Do not accept questionable gifts.

Fourth line up
Deal with the things that obstruct you now. Happiness is at hand.

Fifth line up
Take a break, withdraw, and let something go. Things are on the mend, so you do not need to worry so much.

Top line
What you thought was an obstacle turns out to be a cause for rejoicing. The bad times are over.

13. T'ung jen. Community.
Upper trigram: Ch'ien. Creativity. Heaven.
Lower trigram: Li. Clinging. Flame.

The Image
Fire begins to rise to the heavens—it is the nature of fire to rise upward. Heaven moves in the same direction as fire, yet it is different from fire. Humanity needs to be organized into groups rather than being a jumble of individuals—there must be order within diversity. This hexagram symbolizes the act of friendship.

Keywords
Assemble, cooperate, unite for a common purpose, harmonize, bring together, share, agree, understanding.

Interpretation
Teamwork is the key to success, although you may need to become leader of the team. There will be competitors and battles but there is light at the end of the tunnel. You will soon

be able to make better progress and pass from obscurity to a brighter and more successful future. Find ways to unite people, and goals that can be shared. Put your ideas to the test. Success is yours, but you must share the benefits with others and work in concert with colleagues if you can.

The Lines

Lowest line

You are about to join a specific group of people. Though this is beneficial, you should keep an eye on deals that are being done behind your back.

Second line up

Learn from the mistakes of others and ensure that you are seeing things clearly. Avoid getting involved with a group that has shady motives.

Third line up

Stop, think, and find help. You are facing a strong antagonist, so you may be unable to act for a while.

Fourth line up

No one can attack or control you, and you are no longer boxed in. You cannot fight, but you will see other ways around your problem.

Fifth line up

Having a cause unites people. Using sincere words brings the group together. Acknowledge your bond with another, and remain true to your partner.

Top line

People are gathering together but they have no sense of purpose. You can join in and hope that something good emerges.

14. Ta yu. Wealth.

Upper trigram: Li. Clinging. Flame.
Lower trigram: Ch'ien. Creativity. Heaven.

The Image

The fire in heaven above shines far and wide, so everything stands out in the light and becomes real and solid. Light pours over the earth and illuminates both good and evil. The two trigrams in this hexagram indicate that strength and clarity unite.

Keywords

Possession, success, big, noble, important, time to be great, able to protect others, own, sharing.

Interpretation

You will soon be successful but you may incur jealousy. Small losses may occur through not watching your pennies closely enough. Riches, wealth, and success are assured. An initial setback will be overcome and success will follow. Work and study will go together, and you will soon be in a better position to understand the tasks ahead of you. Do not go overboard trying to impress people but gently convert them to your ideas. Show respect for others and be wary of becoming lazy and arrogant, otherwise you risk losing what you have. Grasp the basics and get on with the job quietly. Act wisely now and all will be well.

The Lines

Lowest line
You may wonder if your hard work is worthwhile. You are laying a good foundation, so nothing that you are doing is a waste of energy. Be aware of your problems so that you can work on them.

Second line up
You need a clear direction but you will cope with responsibility once you know where you are going. People will give you the help that you need.

Third line up
Concentrate on what you have achieved. Do not allow trivial matters to weigh on your mind. Be prepared to share what you have with others.

Fourth line up
Do not try to dominate the situation. Share what you have and allow others to shine. Avoid envy and the temptation to compete.

Fifth line up
You will meet people and you will impress them. Stay true to your ideas but do not be dogmatic or obstinate.

Top line
You have a winning idea, but when success comes do think of others as well as yourself.

15. Ch'ien. Modesty.
Upper trigram: K'un. Receptivity. Earth.
Lower trigram: Ken. Keeping still. Mountain.

The Image
The wealth that is upon or inside the mountain is not visible. The path to your particular goal may seem long and winding, but it all comes clear once you reach your destination. Lowliness is a quality of the earth but in this case, the earth is placed above the mountain. This suggests that a modest attitude is best for the time being.

Keywords
Modest, polite, simple, respectful, yielding, and compliant.

Interpretation

Avoid extremes and try to achieve a balance in your life. Keep thing simple and stick to the facts. Be modest but not stupidly humble, and do not allow yourself to become a victim. The best relationships are those that are on an equal footing. Sometimes you need to give way to others in order to restore the balance. You do not need to shout about your achievements because they will gain recognition anyway. Things are approaching completion. You have the power to shape your fate and to choose the kind of behavior that will bring success.

The Lines

Lowest line

Think everything through twice and develop a sense of purpose. Your task will be easier if you get down to it now.

Second line up

Try out your ideas. By making a heartfelt statement you can get what you want.

Third line up

Do not push yourself forward too much, just carry on quietly. You will be criticized if you sing your own praises too loudly.

Fourth line up

Say what you think but do not argue or impose your will. On the other hand do not downplay your own worth.

Fifth line up

Take action. If you do not have sufficient resources, accept help from someone nearby. Do what is necessary.

Top line

Mobilize your forces. If you need something before you can proceed, now is the time to go out and get it.

16. Yu. Enthusiasm.
Upper trigram: Chen. Arousing. Thunder.
Lower trigram: K'un. Receptivity. Earth.

The Image
Electrical energy comes rushing forth and the thunderstorm refreshes nature. Tension is released and there is a feeling of relief. You can expect joy and heartfelt enthusiasm.

Keywords
Prepare, take precautions, arrange, make ready, happy, be content, rejoice, take pleasure, enthusiasm, and spontaneity.

Interpretation
Muster enthusiasm and prepare for a new project. You have plenty of energy. Ensure that all is in order and that there are no loose ends before you make a start. There are people who will help you. You will need to advertise yourself and to create an enthusiastic atmosphere, but do not fall for your own propaganda. Take opportunities as they arise and act with conviction, but make sure you do not appear overconfident or arrogant. Consider the needs of others.

The Lines
Lowest line
Create an enthusiastic atmosphere but do not leave others to do all the hard work. Do not boast.
Second line up
You are limiting yourself and you may be deluding yourself as well. Be firm, quit if you have to, and do not allow illusions to mislead you.
Third line up
Do not be skeptical or doubtful. Do not procrastinate. Do what needs to be done and seize the moment.

Fourth line up
You can acquire what you want. Your sincerity and confidence draws others to you.

Fifth line up
You are confronting affliction, sickness, or hatred. Keep calm and keep going. Ironically, the things that hold you back will do you a favor because they will stop you from rushing in and doing something foolish.

Top line
Let go of what is past. Although the situation is not your fault, you do not have to let it continue.

17. Sui. Following.
Upper trigram: Tui. Joy. Lake.
Lower trigram: Chen. Arousing. Thunder.

The Image
Thunder in the middle of the lake serves as the image. It is a time of darkness and rest. Electricity withdraws into the earth. After being hard at work all day, you can allow yourself a good rest and recuperation.

Keywords
Some kind of sequence or order of things. Conform to, according to, in the style of.

Interpretation
Let go of what is past, because a new focus is emerging. This is a good time for intimate relationships but not for business affairs. Having said this, it is possible to make new friends at this time. At work it is best to drift with the current and to allow others to show you the way or to take the initiative on your behalf. You will be in charge of your own affairs again soon enough. Adapt, be consistent, make progress, and succeed.

The Lines

Lowest line
Leave your dyed-in-the-wool opinions behind. You need to listen to others and to blend in.

Second line up
You may be taking responsibility for something that is not your problem or wasting energy on unworthy or thankless friends.

Third line up
Accept your responsibilities and you can get where you want to be. Avoid being led astray by silly people with frivolous ideas.

Fourth line up
The path you are following is not going anywhere. You need to change your approach. People may try to take advantage of you.

Fifth line up
You are moving towards something really worthwhile but you need to believe in yourself and in your goal.

Top line
You hold others together and they will call upon you for help. However, for the time being you can only follow. Right now, leadership is not for you.

18. Ku. Decay.
Upper trigram: K'en. Keeping still. Mountain.
Lower trigram: Sun. Gentleness. Wind.

The Image
The wind blows and bounces off the mountain, then it blows down the mountain again. This double whammy can spoil crops and vegetation. This hexagram suggests that change and movement may be needed, but it will not be accomplished without a few hiccups. You need to avoid taking attitudes that could destroy what you are trying to achieve.

Keywords
Rotting, poisonous, seduce, pervert, flatter, and enchant, disorder, error.

Interpretation
There is a choice to be made that could lead to success or failure. Losses, setbacks, and hardships surround you. Whatever is on your mind could lead to trouble, so a change in attitude will help. Take time to think over your decisions, act carefully, and avoid new commitments at this time. If you find the source of the problem, you can stop the rot, stabilize the situation, and bring some form of undeveloped potential into being. Taking care will produce success, although there is still some risk of failure. Something has gone wrong and it must be put right, and you may have to apologize for a mistake or sort out a misunderstanding. You need to be scrupulously honest in all your dealings. It will take some effort but you can make a new start on something now. You will soon be busy again. Avoid decisions on partnerships or marriage at this time.

The Lines
Lowest line
Take advice from others in this difficult time, but accept that some people in authority may be dishonest.

Second line up
Gentle consideration is called for. Do not hurt others by taking drastic action.

Third line up
If you bend over backward to adapt to a new situation you will regret it, so stick to your own ideas and finish what you have started.

Fourth line up
If you continue in the way you have been, you will end up confused and ashamed. Problems that have their roots in the past have to be dealt with.

Fifth line up
Use praise when dealing with others. You can gain status and authority and achieve your aim. Even if you cannot create a new beginning, you can obtain help to change things for the better.

Top line
Not everyone needs to become involved in the affairs of the world, so it may be better for you to sit things out and to allow the world to go its own way for a while. You need to consider life and also to look inside yourself to see what is worthwhile.

19. Lin. Gathering strength.
Upper trigram: K'un. Receptivity. Earth.
Lower trigram: Tui. Joyous. Lake.

The Image
The earth is higher than the lake. This symbolizes the help that those in a high position give to those beneath. The lake is immeasurably deep, so a wise person is always ready and able to teach humanity.

Keywords
Approach, make contact, come closer, confer favor.

Interpretation
You need to deal kindly with those who are under your control. You are (or you soon will be) in an excellent position in life, so this is the time to be generous to others. Follow the advice you are offered. Remain firm in your convictions. Your troubles will diminish and recognition will follow, with many benefits becoming available if you treat others kindly and with modesty. Problems are indicated later, so your success may be short-lived. The best thing to do is to enjoy success while it

lasts. You need to work determinedly to make the best use of this time.

The Lines

Lowest line

You are about to make an influential connection. Do not get carried away by what is happening right now but stick to what you know to be right.

Second line up

An influential person or connection will help you. You do not need to worry about the future because you will realize that your present difficulties are only temporary.

Third line up

You may be too easygoing in your dealings with others. Be aware of your responsibilities, and ensure that other people do not shirk theirs.

Fourth line up

Things are coming to a head, so this is the time to push for what you want.

Fifth line up

Those who know the score will help you to make the right decisions, but you must ensure that you surround yourself with the right people.

Top line

You can expect a windfall and also generosity from others. Do not sit around now because this is a time to be active and to go out into the world. Those whom you teach and help will gain much from you.

20. Kuan. Contemplating.
Upper trigram: Sun. Gentleness. Wind.
Lower trigram: K'un. Receptivity. Earth.

The Image
The wind blows far and wide over the face of the earth, and grass must bend to its power. Your mere existence and the impact of your personality can sway people to your way of seeing things. The wind blowing over the earth represents the kind of regular journeys that you need to make in order to obtain the knowledge that you need before you can act effectively.

Keywords
Contemplate, look from a distance, have perspective, judge, point out, make known.

Interpretation
The immediate future is difficult. You will feel as though you are being blown around and are unable to achieve anything. The situation will improve, but you need to be patient. This is not necessarily a good time in which to take action, because you need to look around for ideas and to gain more insight. Now is a good time to undertake a course of study or to begin training and keep your eyes open for opportunities. You also need to be aware of the wider issues. Things will change spontaneously. Do not take anything on trust; allow your intuition to kick in and to be your guide.

The Lines
Lowest line
Do not just think of yourself. Look around at the less obvious aspects of your situation. You may need to plan ahead rather than just taking things as they come.

Second line up
If you are in a position of responsibility make sure that you are above reproach. You need to learn how to put yourself in another's place.

Third line up
Examine your life and decide whether or not to act. Pay attention to the effects that your actions have on the lives of those around you.

Fourth line up
Take advantage of your position because you are now in a situation where you can use your influence.

Fifth line up
Think of others and do not act in a self-centered way.

Top line
Do not put the blame on others, even if they appear to be complete fools. You share with them some of the responsibility for what is going on.

21. Shih Ho. Biting through.
Upper Trigram: Li. Fire.
Lower trigram: Chen. Thunder.

The Image
Two powerful but opposing forces cause a massive buildup of power and a great noise. Eventually there will be a release as the storm breaks and puts out the fire.

Keywords
Change, reform, transformation, breaking past links, renewal.

Interpretation
Look inside yourself and see what needs to be changed, because a change of attitude might be just what you need. Perhaps you need a change of environment or to leave behind

familiar situations that have now become uncomfortable or unhappy. You may need to enforce the rules so that others start to behave properly. You can improve personal relationships by talking things over and by clearing up misunderstandings. Do not back off from a fight and do not stay put and take things lying down any longer.

The Lines

Lowest line

If you have forgotten how to tell right from wrong, you will soon be shown the error of your ways.

Fifth line up

Stop and think before making decisions, as the wrong choice will land you in hot water.

Fourth line up

You are not in a position of strength, so it will be extremely hard for you to transform the situation, but you must do it anyway.

Third line up

Your task may be hard, but you must not give up. Someone in a powerful position is standing in your way but as long as you persist, you will get the job done regardless of opposition.

Second line up

There may be a lot of choices in front of you, but the right one will soon become clear. This will help you to make the right decision.

Top line

Something is very wrong here, and it might be you who is at the heart of the problem. If you have strayed from the right path, you must recognize this and put things right.

22. Pi. Grace. Adorning.

Upper trigram: Ken. Keeping still. Mountain.
Lower trigram: Li. Clinging. Fire.

The Image

The light of the fire illuminates the mountain. This looks lovely, but the light cannot shine very far. Important questions cannot be resolved if they are based on how things appear rather than how they really are.

Keywords

Embellish, beautify, elegant, inner worth seen in outer appearance, brave, eager, intrepid, the link between value and beauty.

Interpretation

Be firm but flexible and you will be lucky and happy. Dress well and look successful to sell an idea or promote yourself. You may need to improve your appearance before attending an important event. Look beyond what is in front of you, no matter how attractive those things appear to be. Make everything look as good as possible and adapt to what needs to be done. Once you have achieved your aim, do not live beyond your means. Ensure that you are not looking at any person or situation through rose-colored glasses.

The Lines

Lowest line
Go your own way, be honest, and avoid ostentation.
Second line up
Be brave and patient and bear in mind that things are not quite as they seem. If you judge things wrongly now, you will suffer as a result.
Third line up
Keep persevering, even though things look good now and you may not want to keep on making an effort. There

are one or two serious problems around you that need to be dealt with.

Fourth line up

Things are changing, but the new issues that have arisen will not do you any harm. Make alliances and new friends. You may have to give up some comforts, but the close friendship that is on offer will help you to find peace.

Fifth line up

Do not despair, because things are not as bad as they seem. Your sincerity makes a difference. Be careful to make the right choice now, or you may fall flat on your face.

Top line

Access whatever worthwhile characteristics you may have and rely on your good points. Your mistakes are not deliberate, so you will be forgiven.

23. Po. Instability.
Upper trigram: Ken. Keeping still. Mountain.
Lower trigram: K'un. Receptivity. Earth.

The Image
The mountain rests on the earth. If it is steep and narrow and lacking a broad base, it will eventually topple over. Like the mountain, you need a broad foundation to be secure. You need to be benevolent and generous like the earth that holds us all because only then will you feel secure.

Keywords
Flay, peel, skin, scrape, remove, take off, diminish, reduce to essentials, prune, and take decisive action.

Interpretation

Losses and disappointments surround you. You need to get rid of outmoded ideas and remove those things from your life that are no longer useful. This is a poor time for speculation and business because backstabbing and gossiping abound. Some aspect of your life is being destroyed so that you can build afresh for the future. Guard against people who might undermine you. This is the end of one cycle and it is a time to prepare for something new. You are not being cowardly if you do not do much of anything at this awkward time.

The Lines

Lowest line

Change your position and look at things from another point of view. People are trying to undermine you. Although things look disastrous, there is nothing you can do but wait.

Second line up

Set yourself apart from others and deal with the matter at hand. Be prepared to adapt. The worst is over and things will soon improve.

Third line up

Choose your friends carefully. You may have made ties that are wrong for you.

Fourth line up

Do not do things the way you wish to, because you will hurt yourself and others. It would be better not to get too involved in other people's business.

Fifth line up

Opposing forces can unite for mutual benefit. Take the advice that is on offer to you.

Top line

Stay calm when things fall apart. Better times will come along soon.

24. Fu. Turning point.

Upper trigram: Kun. Receptivity. Earth.
Lower trigram: Chen. Arousing. Thunder.

The Image

In winter, the energy of life that is symbolized by thunder is still underground. Things are just beginning to move, but the land must rest so that nothing grows or develops prematurely. You need to renew your energy by resting.

Keywords

Turn back, reappear, rebirth, reestablish, renew, restore, and retrace a path.

Interpretation

A change of season brings improvements and a renewal of energy. Be patient, because improvements are on their way and everything is about to be reborn. Reunions are likely. Your current troubles, sadness, and confusion will give way to improvements that are already happening, even though you cannot yet see them. Things have been delayed, but the turning point will soon come and things will happen when they are meant to.

The Lines

Lowest line

Do not go too far away or put off getting back on time from a trip. You could all too easily miss something important.

Second line up

Let go of what you are doing and be unselfish. What you gain will far outweigh any losses.

Third line up

You must face a ghost from your past. If you find yourself facing the same person or in the same situation as before, you will repeat your previous actions. You may

not be able to reestablish a relationship because you may
need to be on your own for a while.

Fourth line up

Go back to where you were, maybe even to your parents'
home, if that is the best option. If you have to live or
work alone for a while, so be it. Things will soon change
for the better.

Fifth line up

Windfalls, benefits, and generosity are on the way now.
You may have to return to some past destination. If
someone challenges you, do not offer them trivial
excuses. Something new is on the way.

Top line

Retreat, think a while, and start again. Be prepared to
find the right moment to return. Avoid being obstinate.

25. Wu Wang. Innocence.

Upper trigram: Ch'ien. Creativity. Heaven.
Lower trigram: Chen. Arousing. Thunder.

The Image

In springtime when thunder starts below the heavens,
everything sprouts and grows and you must go back to a more
innocent time.

Keywords

Caught up in, entangled, enmeshed, vain, rash, reckless,
foolish, wild, lie, deceive, futile, false, disordered.

Interpretation

Do not rush into anything without thinking. Be honest
and stay within your own limitations. Be unselfish and
uncomplicated and do not let temporary setbacks upset you.
Be ready for unexpected events and be flexible in the way that
you handle them. Follow the directions given by someone you

respect and good fortune will follow. Be spontaneous and free yourself from obsessive ideas and emotions. If you do not look into things before you act, you will make mistakes through ignorance. Beware of getting caught up in other people's messes. Act as though you were an innocent child— that is, naturally, honorably, and truthfully, without greed, ambition, or desire.

The Lines

Lowest line

Do not get entangled. Abandon the present situation and accept that it is at an end. Follow your intuition.

Second line up

This is not the right time to push for something. Just do what you have to do and do not worry about the outcome.

Third line up

The present problem is not yours and neither is it your fault, so do not get involved. You need to accommodate yourself to whatever is demanded of you. Trust your feelings.

Fourth line up

You cannot lose what really belongs to you, even if you throw it away. All you need to do is remain true to yourself.

Fifth line up

The mess that is surrounding you is not your fault. Let nature take its course. Things will soon change.

Top line

Stay uninvolved and do as little as possible. The time is not ripe for action, so it is best to wait quietly. You will not succeed by acting thoughtlessly.

26. Ta Ch'u. Great accumulating.

Upper trigram: Ken. Keeping still. Mountain.
Lower trigram: Ch'ien. Creativity. Heaven.

The Image

Heaven within the mountain points to hidden treasures. Some kind of treasure is hidden in the words and deeds of the past—perhaps some kind of legacy. Whatever it is, you can use it to your advantage. The riches of the past offer you something that you can apply to improve your current situation—even if this is something intangible like knowledge or a particular qualification.

Keywords

Big, noble, important, able to protect others, self-imposed goal, gather, collect, hoard, retain, control, support, tolerate, tame.

Interpretation

You will shortly be able to make great advances in your career. Putting your ideas to the test brings profit and insight, so do not hold back—take action. Hard work and steady progress will bring success. Difficulties will be overcome and even awkward people can be used to your advantage. You need to win over rather than subdue those who oppose you. You can realize your hidden potential because you already have the inner strength and wisdom that you will need when stepping out on your new path. Current obstacles will slip away, but small ones will come into view. You may get involved in community activities at this time.

The Lines

Lowest line
Turn down the challenge and move away from what might become a disaster. Circumstances are holding you back now, but the obstacles will soon disappear.

Second line up
Relationships have broken down. Do not try to compete. If you get to the heart of the problem you can resolve it.
Third line up
Accept that you have a period of boring work or drudgery ahead of you. Doing this will free your mind and enable you to try out a few ideas. The main obstacle that lies in your path has been removed, but you should guard against further problems.
Fourth line up
Gather your strength, because soon you will have to carry heavy loads and confront difficult situations.
Fifth line up
An old enemy cannot harm you. Stop relying on others. Sometimes it is better to be indirect in what you do and say.
Top line
Do not envy others. If there is something you want to do or have, you can get it for yourself.

27. I. Nourishment.
Upper trigram: Ken. Keeping still. Mountain.
Lower trigram: Chen. Arousing. Thunder.

The Image
In spring, the fields are made ready for the time when the seeds are to be sown. This is an image of providing nourishment through movement and tranquility. You can nourish your character in the same way. When you are tranquil, you do not say too much (or the wrong thing!). This will help you develop a nicer nature.

Keywords
Mouth, eat, feed, nourish, sustain, and provide what is necessary.

Interpretation

You need to take in what has happened and use your knowledge to nourish new thoughts, ideas, and projects. Nourish and encourage others now. Give some thought to your loved ones and help those who work for you. Beware of using people. Consider your words carefully. This is a time for rest and relaxation and building up your strength for the future.

The Lines

Lowest line

Do what you have to do, and do not envy others. If you show jealousy or resentment, others will sneer at you.

Second line up

You are lacking something that you need and feel unable to value or support yourself. You can be independent, so do not ask others to prop you up.

Third line up

You are turning your back on something that will help you to grow and develop. Do not go in for short-term gratification but help others and give to charity.

Fourth line up

Your efforts have the effect of brightening up your life. You need others to help you so that you can be your best.

Fifth line up

Reject foolish rules and regulations. Do not move around, but stay where you are and test your ideas. You know your own shortcomings.

Top line

Now you can confront an angry ghost from your past. You need to deal with your responsibilities.

28. Ta Kuo. The great.

Upper trigram: Tui. Joyous. Lake.

Lower trigram: Sun. Gentleness. Wind

The Image

At times a lake can overflow and drown a forest, but the trees stand firm and emerge undamaged after the flood has passed. You may need to turn away from the world for a while, almost as if you are temporarily under the water, but you will soon emerge with a smile on your face.

Keywords

Big, noble, important, able to protect others, self-imposed goal, go beyond, surpass, overtake and surmount difficulties.

Interpretation

Taking on too much will stretch you to the breaking point. Accept your limitations and work within them. You may be working too hard. Avoid jumping into something new, because the current situation will soon improve. If there is an escape route open to you, use it now. Do not be arrogant or aggressive. Be wary if you are thinking of taking up with a younger lover or rescuing a person who has problems. Do not be afraid to strike out on your own.

The Lines

Lowest line

Prepare carefully, be clear about where you are going, and concentrate on the essentials. This goal is worthwhile.

Second line up

Although the action you take may be unusual, it will work out well. You may feel tired and in need of rest.

Third line up
You cannot continue to prop up the current situation, and the harder you try the worse it will get. You can still achieve a lot by accepting help from others.

Fourth line up
Do not try to go any further; take a break if you need to. Misusing your power will only land you in trouble, so do not be obstinate.

Fifth line up
Do not snub those who are in a lower position than you, or you will lose out and cause some kind of instability.

Top line
Think carefully and choose the level at which you want to become involved. Something larger than obvious everyday matters is going on here.

29. K'an. Water. A ravine, danger.

Upper trigram: K'an. The abyss. Water.
Lower trigram: K'an. The abyss. Water.

The Image

Water reaches its goal by flowing without stopping, and it fills up every depression in the ground before it flows on. Similarly, you should strive to do the right thing by design rather than allowing good things to happen by accident. Consistency is important.

Keywords

Danger, pit, critical time, test, take risks without worrying about it.

Interpretation

There are some nasty pitfalls ahead, accompanied by a warning of danger. If you must take a risk, then do it, but it would be better to leave things alone. Conserve your energy, because you will need it when you have to face the dangers that lie ahead. Be careful and patient. Guard against theft, trickery, and the misuse of alcohol. Women may have female problems. Keep the lines of communication open and act according to your principles. When confronted with problems you must do what you know to be the right thing, because then you can reach the heart of the situation. Do what needs to be done and leave risky ventures for another time.

The Lines

Lowest line

Avoid bad habits and do not do anything in a sloppy manner. Do not accept sloppiness in yourself or others.

Second line up

Be flexible; look around for what you need. Calmly weigh up necessities and take things one step at a time.

Third line up

You will not achieve anything if you do not know what you want. Do not be misled into action; wait until the time is right.

Fourth line up

Act with sincerity and be prepared to go it alone. Begin with the things that you understand and the rest will become easier.

Fifth line up

Do not make a great fuss or overdo things. Stay out of harm's way, and avoid being too ambitious.

Top line

If you continue doing what you are doing, you will not get anywhere. If you have been in the wrong crowd or living a bad lifestyle, you will suffer the consequences of your actions.

30. Li. Clinging fire.
Upper trigram: Li. Clinging. Flame.
Lower trigram: Li. Clinging. Flame.

The Image
Each of the two trigrams represents the sun during the course of a day. The bright sunlight allows you to see farther and also more deeply.

Keywords
Light, warmth, fire, illuminate, discriminate, articulate, arranger, awareness, separate self from, step outside the norm, encounter by chance, adhere to, depend on.

Interpretation
You are becoming more aware. Clear your mind and think logically and dispassionately about your life and your problems. Intellectual pursuits will go well, and a thoughtful approach to anything will be helpful. Passion may rule your head for a while, so you need to apply common sense. Recognizing your own limitations will help you to reach for success.

The Lines
Lowest line
Do not be misled—be aware of the motives of others. Avoid being swept along, and act with reserve and composure.
Second line up
A reasonable attitude is necessary. Be clear in your own mind about what you want to happen.
Third line up
Do not dwell on the downside of the situation, because the problem is only temporary. Do not overreact to your situation or waste time worrying about it.

Fourth line up
Although things are good now, they may not stay that way because changes are inevitable.

Fifth line up
Grief at the end of a relationship may seem never ending, but there are benefits to be found. Try to maintain a balanced attitude.

Top line
Root out your bad habits and rid yourself of them. Something new is about to begin in your life.

31. Hsien. Relating, attraction.
Upper trigram: Tui. Joyous. Lake.
Lower trigram: K'en. Keeping still. Mountain

The Image
A mountain with a lake at its summit. The moisture from the lake irrigates the mountain. Be open to new ideas and do not become big-headed or opinionated, so you will be receptive to good advice in the same way that the mountain receives drops of water from the lake.

Keywords
Contact, influence, move, excite, mobilize, trigger, entire, unite.

Interpretation
Attraction will bring people together. This could be the start of a blissful love affair or a successful business partnership. Try to discover why you are attracted to someone or what that person wants before becoming too involved with him or her. Be sensitive to their needs while still being yourself. A little flexibility now could open the door to a new relationship. Choose your moment to act carefully.

The Lines

Lowest line
It may be difficult to see what you are supposed to be doing, but look around and see if you can work it out for yourself.

Second line up
Wait quietly until you need to act and then apply the right amount of effort at the right time.

Third line up
Stay where you are for the time being. Others will come along and show you what you should be doing. Watch your temper now, because your moods are unpredictable.

Fourth line up
You are finding it difficult to make up your mind, but if you think deeply you may be able to reach some kind of decision. Once you have done this, stick with it—and avoid the temptation to manipulate others.

Fifth line up
This will be a good relationship for you, but you must keep your head and not get too carried away at the start.

Top line
Talking is one thing, but it is only when you take some action that the situation will change. Take one step at a time and do not try to solve the whole problem at once.

32. Heng. Persevering.
Upper trigram: Chen. Arousing. Thunder.
Lower trigram: Sun. Gentleness. Wind.

The Image
Thunder and wind are both active, so this hexagram represents the changes that can happen around us from time to time. You must keep abreast of the times and keep an eye on what is going on. Whether you stay as you are or go with the flow will be a matter of judgment.

Keywords

Continuing, constant, stable, regular, durable, permanent, and habitual.

Interpretation

Persevere and allow things to take their course, because rushing ahead brings its own problems. Do not insist on having things all your own way. A relaxed attitude will work better. A difficult situation will come to an end and your relationship will strengthen. Let things happen in their own time.

The Lines

Lowest line

If you want a situation to last, you have to think hard and put some work into it. Keep cool and take things slowly.

Second line up

Your regrets will soon be behind you. Apply the right amount of effort at the right time.

Third line up

Your moods are unpredictable, and if you let them control your actions, your inconsistency will cause problems.

Fourth line up

Take what you need and slip quietly away without making a fuss.

Fifth line up

Choose how you want to continue. If something dishonest or deceitful is going on, cut yourself off from the situation in order to preserve your integrity.

Top line

Rushing at things will do more harm than good. Do not try to change everything overnight.

33. Tun. Retreat.
Upper trigram: Ch'ien. Creativity. Heaven.
Lower trigram: Ken. Keeping still. Mountain.

The Image
The mountain rises upward, pushing against the lower reaches of heaven, but heaven retreats and remains out of touch. This symbolizes the way you can retreat into your own thoughts. Dignified reserve makes a good weapon.

Keywords
Withdraw, run away, escape, hide, and be antisocial.

Interpretation
The best course of action will be to withdraw in the face of conflict. This does not mean that you will be running away from a situation; you are wisely avoiding confrontation with those who oppose you. It may be advisable to keep certain people at a distance for a while. Sometimes you have to step back before you can make a fresh move. Business is not good now, and you must not throw good money after bad. Do not embark on a relationship or anything new at this time. You need to conserve your energy and consolidate existing ventures with care. Avoid getting into a power struggle. Some people may seek to take advantage of you. Do not try to impose your ideas on others. When the right moment comes for you to take power into your own hands and make your move, be sure that you do not miss the opportunity.

The Lines
Lowest line
Stay where you are for the time being, and if you have retreated to a place of safety, stay put.
Second line up
Do not let anything pry you loose. Stay firm and do not give up the struggle—then you will reach your goal.

Third line up
You cannot manage alone, but it is hard to know on whom you can rely. Ensure that no one gets in your way or holds you back.

Fourth line up
By retreating, you can hold fast to your convictions. You are stuck in the midst of a tough situation.

Fifth line up
There is no doubt that you are right, but nevertheless, you should keep your opinions to yourself for a while and maintain a calm and friendly attitude.

Top line
Your doubts will disappear when your future path becomes clear. Your depression and anger will fade when you can see where you should be going.

34. Ta Chuang. Great power.
Upper trigram: Chen. Arousing. Thunder.
Lower trigram: Ch'ien. Creativity. Heaven.

The Image
The spring brings the first thunderstorms, and these produce great power. Greatness depends on being in harmony with what is right, so you should avoid doing anything that is not in harmony with the established order.

Keywords
Big, important, inspire, animate, strengthen, drive, mature, damage, wound, unrestrained use of strength.

Interpretation
This is a time of progress when others follow your example, so act justly and wisely and follow your actions through to the end. Be prepared to take the initiative and make an effort to succeed, but do not be forceful when it is not

necessary. Avoid throwing your weight around or being too one-sided. If you have to use strong words, be prepared to back them with action. Wait until the moment is right before you act.

The Lines

Lowest line

You can burn yourself out if you act too quickly. You are tempted to force your way forward, but this would lead to trouble.

Second line up

Put your plan to the test and then persevere with it. Any remaining resistance to your aims will soon fade away.

Third line up

You do not need to use force, and pushing too hard will bring trouble. Blowing your own horn will not do you any good at all.

Fourth line up

Persevere now and you will soon find that obstacles clear away. Just keep quietly plugging away.

Fifth line up

Changes are going on around you that will offer new opportunities. Insisting on retaining the status quo or behaving in a stubborn or belligerent manner will not get you anywhere.

Top line

You have to deal with your responsibilities, but stay within the parameters in which you find yourself. There is a kind of deadlock here, which is making it hard for you to advance or retreat.

35. Chin. Progress.
Upper trigram: Li. Clinging. Flame.
Lower trigram: K'un. Receptivity. Earth.

The Image
The light of the sun rises above the earth, spreading its rays over an ever-widening area. This shows that things are improving. Your nature is basically good, but you may be behaving in a less-than-perfect manner due to the things that are going on around you. Center yourself and make sure that you are pure in heart. Be ready to give and receive.

Keywords
Prosper, grow, flourish, advance, increase, progress, be promoted, and rise.

Interpretation
Things are improving and you are on the way up, so this is an excellent time for success at work, but you must be fair and modest in order to succeed. You need to think of others as well as yourself. Communication is important and you should avoid acting aggressively. Take delight in what you already have. People will rally around you, and they will be willing to follow your lead.

The Lines
Lowest line
Be generous and act independently. Do what you know is right, and do not worry if others disagree or ostracize you as a result.
Second line up
Accept the sorrow that your situation brings. Happiness will come soon. Take on responsibilities with compassion and intelligence.

Third line up
People have confidence in you, but you must not be underhanded if you want to keep it.

Fourth line up
Do not focus on obtaining money or possessions right now. If there is an obstacle to your progress, it will soon disappear. If you need to start something new, you will also need to leave behind something old.

Fifth line up
You will not regret acting now, but you cannot do everything until you have removed one particular obstacle.

Top line
Use your strength carefully, you cannot move forward just yet. Keep calm and have faith.

36. Ming I. Darkening of the light.
Upper trigram: K'un. Receptivity. Earth.
Lower trigram: Li. Clinging. Flame.

The Image
In times of darkness you need to be cautious and reserved because you will upset others and make enemies if you behave in an inconsiderate manner. The flame brings the earth's darkness into the light, but you do not need to shine your own light too brightly.

Keywords
Prosper, grow, flourish, advance, increase, progress, be promoted, rise, and permeate.

Interpretation
Do not be downhearted if things are not going well. There is no need to be tossed around by your problems. Be careful about whom you trust, and act cautiously. Be patient

because things will improve. Keep your opinions to yourself and try to not take on too much for a while. You need to play your cards close to your chest and not give away secrets. Make plans, but try to hide your disappointment until things change for the better. It is best to be subtle in your approach.

The Lines

Lowest line
You need to compromise to overcome your obstacles. Use a little force if necessary. Bad times will soon come to an end.

Second line up
However much you are hurting, you should still put the needs of others above your own. You may soon have to take on extra responsibilities.

Third line up
Even if you have to remove someone abusive from your orbit, do not do this too quickly because some aspects of your situation are worth keeping. If something is not working for you, drop it rather than persisting.

Fourth line up
You need to leave the scene of disaster before the storm breaks. There is no longer any hope of improvement.

Fifth line up
Hide your true abilities until things are clearcr. You cannot progress until the obstacle has been removed.

Top line
Persist until you can see the whole picture. You cannot move forward yet, so keep calm and have faith in yourself.

37. Chia Jen. Family.
Upper trigram: Sun. Gentleness. Wind.
Lower trigram: Li. Clinging. Flame.

The Image
A fire becomes fiercer when the wind blows, so the effect of the wind becomes more obvious to those who are looking at the fire. If you have something to say, ensure that you make sense in the light of reality and present circumstances. Also, ensure that this is not all talk and that your words are backed up by your deeds.

Keywords
Home, family, relations, school of thought, holding something in common, and humanity.

Interpretation
All aspects of family relationships are highlighted. You cannot do anything in isolation but only in coordination with close family and friends. What goes on in a household is a microcosm of what goes on in the world at large, so take note of how these mechanisms work. Behave morally, justly, and with respect for others. In work situations, treat those who are on lower rungs of the ladder as you would like to be treated. Give your superiors the deference they deserve, because at this time it is best to stick to tradition and not try to buck the system.

The Lines
Lowest line
Where all kinds of relationships are concerned, stay within the boundaries and stick to the rules.
Second line up
Do what needs to be done, but avoid giving in to impulses and pushing too hard.

Third line up
You may have to keep others in line, but you must try to strike a balance. If there is a choice, it would be better to be too severe rather than too weak.

Fourth line up
You need to balance what you give against what you receive. Follow the middle path.

Fifth line up
Act from the heart and show your affection. Stick to your values and you will achieve your goals.

Top line
Take responsibility willingly and ensure that everyone knows what they are supposed to be doing.

38. K'ui. Opposition.
Upper trigram: Li. Clinging. Flame.
Lower trigram: Tui. Joyous. Lake.

The Image
Fire and water never mingle because even when they are in contact, they retain they their own natures. In the same way, you can preserve your individuality while joining with others. You can spend time with others without being dragged into dishonorable behavior.

Keywords
Oppose, separate, distant, at odds, discordant, contrary, exclusive, unusual perspective.

Interpretation
Treat others generously if you need to turn conflict and suspicion into shared success. The differences between opposing views are small, and you may have more in common than you think. Try to be constructive and seek harmony. You are not always right, so allow others some leeway, but even

when you are right there is no need to harp on it. Colleagues and family members may see things differently than you. Cooperate as much as you can and wait for this phase to pass. Being quiet and fitting in could be your best tactic for the time being.

The Lines

Lowest line
Do not get entangled in the twisted emotions of others. You cannot force people to like each other. Misunderstandings can cause confusion.

Second line up
By chance, you will meet someone who can help you and working together will bring you good fortune.

Third line up
You cannot get anywhere at the moment and you will feel isolated.

Fourth line up
Although you feel alone, you meet someone whom you can trust completely. You can see a way through all of your problems.

Fifth line up
A sincere person will come along and help you to sort things out. You have no need to look back with regret.

Top line
Do not misjudge your friends or defend yourself against them. They have good intentions, and when you wake up to this, things will be better.

39. Chien. Obstruction.
Upper trigram: K'an. Abyss. Water.
Lower trigram: Ken. Keeping still. Mountain.

The Image
Water on the mountain represents the obstacles that you face. This is an image of a dangerous abyss lying before you and a steep, inaccessible mountain rising behind you, so it symbolizes how obstacles surround you. The mountain does not move so there is a chance that you can find some way around it and overcome the obstacles that stand in your way.

Keywords
Proceed haltingly, difficulties, obstacles, obstructions, unhappy, suffering, afflicted, poverty.

Interpretation
Difficulties surround you, but these are part of an essential process, so try to find a way around your problem rather than moaning about it. Be constant in your objectives but do not apply force to achieve them. It is important to be patient and to think before acting. A direct approach may not be what you need. Try to look at things in a different way. Retreat and get help from others where you can. This is a particularly bad time for relationships. You need to join with those who think as you do and who can show you a way around your problem. Keep going even when circumstances seem to be making it hard to reach your goal. In some way, a temporary obstruction may actually do you a favor as clearing it may make you stronger.

The lines

Lowest line
Difficulties are passing and praise is coming, but you still have to wait. Ask for help and you will get it.

Second line up
Do not doubt yourself; act as straightforwardly as possible. You need to be singleminded to succeed.

Third line up
You will soon have a reason to be happy. Ask for and accept help whenever you need it.

Fourth line up
You cannot manage this situation singlehandedly. You may have to abandon your present plans and seek a new way of doing things.

Fifth line up
You cannot avoid your problem, but help is available. Take it and try to keep your fears under control.

Top line
You cannot turn your back on the current situation, but there is helpful advice on hand, so you can cope.

40. Hsieh. Liberation.
Upper trigram: Chen. Arousing. Thunder.
Lower trigram: K'an. Abyss. Water.

The Image
A thunderstorm clears the air. You may need to put a few things right in order to calm the situation down. Mistakes happen, but you should not dwell on them because they die away like thunder. You can forgive others in the same way that water washes everything clean.

Keywords
Release, solve problems, dispel sorrows, divide, detach, sever, dissolve, analyze and understand, free.

Interpretation
Tensions are beginning to ease, and you can make your way back to a more comfortable situation. Once you have

freed yourself from your current problems, things will improve. The situation will come to a head, and you will know where you stand. Then you can deal with the situation quickly but also gently. You should remember the lessons you have learned and avoid becoming a slave to the past. Show leadership at home and work but allow others some leeway. Joining with others will help you to realize your ambitions. If you have unfinished business, leave it unfinished until you feel more capable of dealing with it. Let things go and be ready to forgive others. Periods of sudden change can actually be liberating.

The Lines

Lowest line

There is no need to go on about things because most of your problem is behind you. Tell your enemies to get lost.

Second line up

Test your ideas but make sure that you use the right methods. You need to rid yourself of your own bad habits.

Third line up

You are at fault and your carelessness might bring you trouble. Tell people who act like parasites to leave you alone.

Fourth line up

You may need to bring partnerships to an end and go it alone. If you do not, then the situation will get out of control.

Fifth line up

You may feel that there is no way out but there is one—and when people see that you are in earnest, they will stop pressuring you.

Top line

Someone is standing in your way, and you must remove this obstacle.

41. Sun. Decrease.

Upper trigram: Ken. Keeping still. Mountain.
Lower trigram: Tui. Joyous. Lake.

The Image

The lake at the foot of the mountain evaporates a little until it is filled again by rainfall. This evaporation benefits the mountain so that it is enriched by its moisture. The mountain represents the strength that can harden into anger, but the lake is the symbol of gaiety, desire, and passion. This suggests that there are times when anger should be curbed, and also that there are times when you need to control your desires, passions, and basic instincts.

Keywords

Lessen, take away, weaken, damage, lose, give away, and offer.

Interpretation

Avoid excesses and preserve what you have, because someone may ensure that you suffer a material loss. You may need to accept a loss but you can easily manage this. You need to redistribute some of your money or goods for the benefit of others. This could even mean a large tax bill. There is no need to be ashamed of poverty or of shortages and managing on less, as this will force you into accepting a simpler lifestyle. Personal relationships may be rather boring, but you should avoid what appear to be exciting emotional entanglements. It is important to curb your anger, keep calm, and avoid excitement for the time being.

The Lines

Lowest line
Bring things to a close and leave quickly. Be ready to offer help where it is needed.

Second line up
You can only help others if you give up some of your own desires. In this case you need to keep your own dignity if you are to be of service to others.

Third line up
A close bond is only possible between two people, while a third brings jealousy. Know your faults and do something about them.

Fourth line up
You are stopping people from getting closer to you. By ridding yourself of your faults you will draw others to your side.

Fifth line up
Fate is ruling your life now, so if you are due for a bit of luck, it will happen no matter what you do.

Top line
What you accomplish is to the benefit of everyone, so improving your life will improve the lives of those who are around you.

42. I. Increase.
Upper trigram: Sun. Gentleness. Wind.
Lower trigram: Chen. Arousing. Thunder.

The Image
Thunder and wind increase and strengthen one another, and this represents your ability to improve yourself and your life. When you see good in others you should imitate them, and when you see faults in yourself do what you can to eradicate those faults.

Keywords
Increase, advance, benefit, strengthen, support, useful, profitable, advantageous.

Interpretation

This is a good time for increased activity and prosperity, so make the most of this period while it lasts. Some of your success is due to luck, rather than ability. Be generous and do not seek unfair advantage over others. Business and finance are improving, and close relationships are working well. You may have to make sacrifices for others. Their happiness and gratitude will make this worthwhile.

The Lines

Lowest line

Use your extra energy to achieve something great. You may try to give others the impression that your motives are unselfish, but they are not as pure as you would like to think they are.

Second line up

Fate is on your side, and your actions can benefit those who are around you. Use this time to do something good for others with no thought of personal gain.

Third line up

Even things that look bad turn out well. Use your power and position wisely to ensure success.

Fourth line up

Do not hold back because of selfishness. Someone else's misfortune brings you luck.

Fifth line up

True kindness and unselfishness on your part will soon be rewarded.

Top line

Neglecting your obligations to others will leave you alone and isolated. You are due for success, so there is no need to be selfish.

43. Kuai. Determination.
Upper trigram: Tui. Joyous. Lake.
Lower trigram: Ch'ien. Creativity. Heaven.

The Image
When the water in a lake evaporates and rises up to heaven it can lead to a cloudburst. This image warns of the violent collapse that could happen when you do not consider others while amassing riches for yourself. As the rain disperses, so must you be generous to others.

Keywords
Decide, declare, resolve, resolute, decisive, stern, certain, settled, separate, flow in different directions.

Interpretation
You must acknowledge the danger that is around you and quietly act against it with the help of others. You will gain more if you act fairly and are cautious about the way you behave. Financial and career matters look good, but it may be wise to take out insurance. Do not allow bad behavior to destroy what you have achieved. There can be no compromise when it comes to removing evil from your life. The best way to combat it is to increase the good in your life. Love affairs are difficult, and quarrels can spoil the atmosphere.

The Lines
Lowest line
Use your energy to achieve something great. You could shoot yourself in the foot by boasting.
Second line up
Be on guard and stay alert. By keeping your wits about you, you will be able to deal with whatever enters your life.

Third line up
Resolve to leave this situation and these people. You are pushing something further than it should go.

Fourth line up
Do not believe everything you're told, but do not be too obstinate to listen to good advice. You may make others angry and resentful.

Fifth line up
You need to be firm and not allow yourself to be deflected. If you need to kick someone, use both feet.

Top line
Communicate with others, and try to avoid making a disastrous mistake that might become an insurmountable setback.

44. Kou. Encountering, temptation.
Upper trigram: Ch'ien. Creativity. Heaven.
Lower trigram: Sun. Gentleness. Wind.

The Image
The wind blows everywhere and it sets heaven in motion. The sun shines, but occasional clouds hide it, symbolizing the way that you can be caught out by temptation when you let down your guard.

Keywords
Encounter, meet, magnetism, enjoyable, sex.

Interpretation
This is a good time to flirt a little and enjoy your social life because you can really enjoy yourself. Serious commitments do not seem to be in the air just now. Business matters are likely to prosper. You should avoid being influenced by others in your work and social life. Beware of dangerous situations. You could suffer from deceit and hidden

agendas. Watch out for your own ulterior motives. Learn from these situations for the future. Calm persuasion will help you to influence others.

The Lines

Lowest line

Find out what is holding you back or entrapping you and remove it. Others may think you are snobbish even though you are not.

Second line up

Do not overspend or use too much credit, because it will make you look weak. Use gentle control rather than violence.

Third line up

Do not let yourself be dragged into something that you feel is not right. There is nothing wrong with showing your feelings.

Fourth line up

Meet people halfway because you may need them later. If you reject them now and they are not there when you need them, it will be your own fault.

Fifth line up

Be alert—both problems and opportunities surround you. There is no need to be stressed about bad fortune or to show off about good luck.

Top line

Do not let a minor problem become a major one. Keep your composure.

45. Ts'ui. Gathering.
Upper trigram: Tui. Joyous. Lake.
Lower trigram: K'un. Receptivity. Earth.

The Image

If the water in the lake gathers until it rises above the earth, there is danger of a breakthrough. If you are prepared for problems to arise you can prevent them. Problems are more likely to occur when a lot of people are brought together. You need to be on guard against the unexpected.

Keywords

Gather, call, group, assemble, collect, concentrate, crowd.

Interpretation

You will soon meet someone who will be important to you. This could be the lover of your dreams or a good business contact. In work situations, you will need harmony and for everybody concerned to make an effort. Uniting for a common purpose will make great things happen. You need a sense of direction. Your sense of calm may be tested, and you should be ready to act if things get out of control. Joining together with others gives you more power.

The Lines

Lowest line
It takes a little effort to turn away stress and to trigger joy. You may try to form a relationship only to be rejected.

Second line up
Choose a strong leader to follow.

Third line up
Work unselfishly for a cause. Although it can be hard to break into a group, there is someone who will help you to do so.

Fourth line up
What you do unselfishly will succeed. Trouble is on the way, but that will soon be put right.

Fifth line up
Your devotion to duty will gain people's confidence. Fate is bringing you a change for the better.

Top line
Your good intentions may be misunderstood. You may feel shy and awkward, but join in group activities anyway.

46. Sheng. Advancing.
Upper trigram: K'un. Receptivity. Earth.
Lower trigram: Sun. Gentleness. Wind.

The Image
The wind adapts itself to obstacles, and it moves onwards and upwards without being stopped and without hurrying. If you keep going, you will do the same.

Keywords
Mount, go up, advance, rise, promote and fulfill potential.

Interpretation
If you have done the groundwork in a situation, it will soon start to take off. Your efforts will be rewarded and creative enterprises will be successful. Avoid arrogance or overconfidence and be prepared to work hard to consolidate your gain. This growth will not continue forever—nothing does—but modesty and flexibility will carry you far.

The Lines

Lowest line
Do not grab a plum job out of selfishness; do the right thing and you will get there anyway.

Second line up
Keep your eye on the ball. Even if you feel that you do not fit in, your sincerity will elicit the right response.

Third line up
This is not the time for doubts and misgivings, as these will only hold you back. Although things look good there is no way of telling how long it will last.

Fourth line up
Dedicate your energy to the good of the group. Find an original or unusual way of doing things.

Fifth line up
Do not let your successes go to your head. Take things a step at a time and you will make calm, steady progress.

Top line
You are on the way up, but you still need to be conscientious and consistent.

47. K'un. Oppression.

Upper trigram: Tui. Joyous. Lake.
Lower trigram: K'an. Abyss. Water.

The Image

When the water has flowed out, the lake will dry up and become exhausted. This symbolizes an adverse period of fate and a time when you need to remain true to yourself.

Keywords

Enclose, restrict, limit, punish, anxiety, fear, fatigue, exhaustion, afflicted, disheartened, weary, poverty.

Interpretation

There will be hard times, probably through fate rather than your own mistakes or stupidity. You may feel cut off from things and need to gather your energy in order to break out and reestablish communication. Do not run away but look inward to find the strength to cope. The losses that you suffer now may be necessary in order to show you what is truly important. Adversity can sometimes be a good thing as it brings out abilities that you do not know you have. Guard against deceit and false flattery.

The Lines

Lowest line

Do not allow past problems to color your future. A negative attitude will hamper your progress.

Second line up

You are bored and you need something new in your life. Be prepared and patient. Obstacles still need to be overcome before you get what you want.

Third line up

You are being indecisive and this will hold you back. Do not magnify small matters or deal with them recklessly.

Fourth line up

Help is slowly coming to you. You are very bored and may need a change in direction.

Fifth line up

You need something worthwhile to work for. Things slowly begin to take a turn for the better.

Top line

Do not dwell on failure or worse will follow. Pull yourself out of the pit of despair in which you have been wallowing.

48. Ching. The well.
Upper trigram: K'an. Abyss. Water.
Lower trigram: Sun. Gentleness. Wind.

The Image
The well benefits everything and everyone. Similarly, you can organize things so that all the separate parts cooperate for the benefit of the whole.

Keywords
Well, resources, underlying structure, nucleus.

Interpretation
If you have to choose between people or between paths, use your intuition and avoid those who are not straight and true. Dig deeply into yourself to find strength from within. Use knowledge that is based on past experience to make sure that you stay on the right path. Things are good at the moment, but you must keep a weather eye out for changes. Although you can change where you live and those with whom you mix, you cannot change your basic needs.

The Lines
Lowest line
You cannot move forward at the moment, but do not allow fear to rule you. Stop wasting your life or others will lose interest in you.

Second line up
You may be stuck but you can ride the situation out. You are neglecting your own good qualities.

Third line up
Not using your capabilities to their fullest extent is one reason why you are unappreciated. You can make small progress now, so do not dwell on the future.

Fourth line up
This is a time of transition, so do not be afraid to act alone. You are at the bottom; the only way you can go now is up.

Fifth line up
Use the talents that you have not bothered to exercise for some time now.

Top line
Get to the bottom of the situation but do not waste time overanalyzing. Get on with things and attend to practical matters.

49. Ko. Revolution.
Upper trigram: Tui. Joyous. Lake.
Lower trigram: Li. Clinging. Flame.

The Image
The fire and lake can fight and destroy one other. Natural evolution means that you have to adjust to the changing demands of the times.

Keywords
Renew, revolt, overthrow, eliminate, repeal, cut away.

Interpretation
Changes are on the way and you may soon change addresses or look for a new job. Divorce, marriage, or even political changes may be in the air, and these will bring good opportunities for you. Try not to be too materialistic. You need to be careful, to reject old motives, settle old quarrels, and act with sincerity. Your manner and presentation will improve and you will soon be able to impress others.

The Lines

Lowest line
Do not make big changes; only small adjustments are needed now.

Second line up
You need to be fully prepared for the major changes that you make.

Third line up
Time your actions well so that you are neither too quick nor too slow. Avoid being selfish or narrowminded.

Fourth line up
Focus on your goals in order to meet them.

Fifth line up
You can make a start now because you have support. It is time to begin something new.

Top line
Do not be impatient. As long as you do not act impulsively, you will be successful.

50. Ting. The cauldron.
Upper trigram: Li. Clinging. Flame.
Lower trigram: Sun. Gentleness. Wind.

The Image
Sun represents wood and wind while *Li* symbolizes flame. Together they stand for the flame kindled by wood and wind—and this suggests the idea of preparing food. The fate of a fire depends on the presence of the wood that will make it burn. Similarly, fate lends power to our lives.

Keywords
Cauldron, sacred vessel for offerings, founding symbol of a family, hold, contain, transform, found, establish, precious, well grounded.

Interpretation

Ensure that your tools, equipment, and vehicles are in good working order so that they will be there for you. Do not worry about small mishaps, but guard against larger ones. Look after your body. This is a time for reflection, because you need to ensure that you have a solid base from which to move.

The Lines

Lowest line

Clearing an obstruction will bring you profit and insight. You will gain recognition for your accomplishments.

Second line up

Success will come as long as you do not throw your weight around.

Third line up

You are feeling unappreciated and ineffective. Tread water now and wait for better times.

Fourth line up

You are not using your talents properly. If someone supports you, treat them well.

Fifth line up

Follow through on your ideas. Others are jealous of your success, but they are not in a position to hurt you.

Top line

Success will be guaranteed as long as you are not too impulsive.

51. Chen. Turmoil.

Upper trigram: Chen. Arousing. Thunder.
Lower trigram: Chen. Arousing. Thunder.

The Image

Thunder bursts forth from the earth causing fear and trembling. This symbolizes how we can be shocked into putting our lives in order.

Keywords

Shock of the new, stirring up, arouse, inspire, wake up, shake up, frighten, awe, alarm, severe, excite, influence, breakthrough.

Interpretation

Stormy weather lies ahead. You should not panic; merely wait until it passes. Repeated shocks are stirring things up and although you feel anxious, good things will come out of this period. Do not lose your concentration. What at first seems frightening will make you happy later. Be wary of problems caused by gossip. Incidentally, this is a good hexagram for anyone who communicates for a living.

The Lines

Lowest line
There could be a shock on the way. You may feel at a disadvantage but this is only temporary.

Second line up
There are difficulties ahead. Do not pursue what you have already lost. You may need to withdraw for a while.

Third line up
Even though you may be shocked into immobility, you still need to act. Your current situation is not appropriate for you.

Fourth line up
Avoid acting compulsively and without thinking things through. Be open to new ideas. This is not the time to take the lead or to be the leader.

Fifth line up
An upheaval can bring loss. Focus on the main issue and you will not get lost.

Top line
The bad times are coming to an end and there is light at the end of the tunnel. Beware of making bad alliances.

52. Ken. Stillness.
Upper trigram: Ken. Keeping still. Mountain.
Lower trigram: Ken. Keeping still. Mountain.

The Image
Two mountains stand together. This symbolizes strength, stillness, and calm.

Keywords
Calm, still, stabilize, articulate, limit, boundary, stop, refuse to advance, enclose, confine, finish, complete, reflect, solid, firm, simple, and straightforward.

Interpretation
Take things easy and move slowly along your present path. Do not take unnecessary gambles; tackle jobs that are more difficult than those that you are already coping with. It is best not to plan too far ahead; simply take things one day at a time. Keep your desires in check and do not act impulsively. You may have to move through your life as if others were not there. Peace, love, and harmony can be expected at home. True quiet means keeping still until the time to take a new path is right. Avoid new partnerships, but be true to existing ones.

The Lines

Lowest line
Make your foundations firm, as this the will help you to build for the future. Your inner strength will help you now.

Second line up
You cannot rescue others, but you can center yourself. Listen to your inner voice.

Third line up
Do not repress your feelings or hide away from others. You can overcome your faults and failings now.

Fourth line up
Relax and meditate. Discover your own inner needs.

Fifth line up
Things are moving slowly, so go with the flow. Be careful—it is all too easy to say something that you will later regret.

Top line
Be generous and kind to others, and your plans will come to completion. Try to maintain an objective attitude.

53. Chien. Gradual advance.
Upper trigram: Sun. Gentleness. Wind.
Lower trigram: Ken. Keeping still. Mountain.

The Image
A tree on a mountain develops slowly and then becomes firmly rooted. This symbolizes slow growth. The tree on the mountain is visible from afar, and its appearance influences the landscape. Its growth proceeds gradually, symbolizing that it sometimes takes time for one's efforts to be recognized.

Keywords

Advance by degrees, pour into, flow into, permeate, influence, affect, smooth, gliding.

Interpretation

Happiness in love or marriage is assured as long as you keep to the rules and do not embark on a fling. Other things develop slowly even though there does not seem much progress at the moment. Do not make sudden changes. Consolidate your gains and allow life to take its course. You achieve your goals by advancing slowly and subtly. Work patiently and gradually toward your objectives. Results will be on a firm foundation, so they should be able to withstand future storms. Plan well, be honest and truthful, and all will be well.

The Lines

Lowest line

You must maintain the achievements you have made so far. Your difficulties will actually help you to achieve success because they prevent you from acting too quickly.

Second line up

You have made progress, but now you need to guard against mistakes. You are ready to share your good fortune with others.

Third line up

Problems are facing you, but you can cope. Avoid provoking arguments and all will be well.

Fourth line up

You will find a useful temporary solution. By yielding and serving others you can adapt to the situation. Take time to relax and think.

Fifth line up
Despite the fact that there is nothing to stop you, you should not try to rush things. Friends will help you. Misunderstandings can be cleared away.

Top line
It is time for a fresh start. Take care to show affection to others.

54. Kuei Mei. The marrying maiden.
Upper trigram: Chen. Arousing. Thunder.
Lower trigram: Tui. Joyous. Lake.

The Image
Thunder stirs the water in the lake and this creates shimmering waves. This indicates that relationships can take wrong turns that may lead to misunderstandings and disagreements. Keep your aims in sight rather than simply drifting along.

Keywords
Return to, change form, retire, revert, become loyal.

Interpretation
Be wary of getting into a situation that you cannot get out of quickly, especially if this involves marrying or becoming entangled in an affair. Try to avoid situations at work and elsewhere in which you are likely to be made the victim. New relationships are doomed to disaster, quarrels, and heartbreak. If you cannot get what you want then at least try to want what you have. Give everything time, because changes may suddenly occur. Even if they do not, you will know that you have given your situation its best shot. Love, sex, and financial decisions are highlighted. Be sure that you are not seduced by something that is superficial or short term,

but look for truth and objectivity. Do not bite off more than you can chew.

The Lines

Lowest line

Accept a secondary position cheerfully because it will lead to eventual success. Give value for money.

Second line up

Take an intelligent perspective. Being alone will offer you insight. Overcome your vanity and pride and avoid acting ostentatiously.

Third line up

Have patience. If you take on a new task now, you will turn the whole situation upside down. Do not take action; sit this one out.

Fourth line up

Wait for the right moment. Compose yourself and concentrate on what you want.

Fifth line up

You are in the center of things. Value your ability to move and act independently. Friends may let you down.

Top line

There is no advantage in clinging to this situation. If the only alternative is to take a low level job then take it anyway. You can always move on to better things later.

55. Feng. Abundance.
Upper trigram: Chen. Arousing. Thunder.
Lower trigram: Li. Clinging. Flame.

The Image

The combination of movement and flame brings clarity. This symbolizes that nothing good lasts forever and that what you have can dissolve or disappear if you are not careful.

Keywords

Fertile, plentiful, copious, exuberant, prolific, overflowing, full, culmination, ripe, sumptuous, luxurious, friends, and riches.

Interpretation

You will be happy, and troubles that come from outside will not be able to harm you. Success, brilliance, and prosperity are indicated, but there is a strong warning not to overexpand or overstep the mark. This is a good time to consolidate your gains, but try not to lay money out on new ventures. Be generous to others. Cut through complications. This is a time to build things up and prepare for hard times that may follow.

The Lines

Lowest line

Someone you admire can help and teach you. You may want more than you can have.

Second line up

Even if you know that you are right, others may not believe you. You cannot solve the present problem, so work around it.

Third line up

Your problems are passing away. If others do not appear to notice you, push yourself forward and make an impact.

Fourth line up

You cannot win every battle—but with a little help from your friends, you can win this one.

Fifth line up

A new chapter in your life will bring you praise and reward. Friends may let you down and bring you disappointment.

Top line
Do not keep things to yourself but join forces with like-minded people. Trying to control others will alienate those to whom you are closest.

56. Lu. Traveling.
Upper trigram: Li. Clinging. Flame.
Lower trigram: Ken. Keeping still. Mountain.

The Image
The mountain stands still, and above it a fire flares up. This symbolizes the separation we can feel from those around us.

Keywords
Travel, quest, journey, visitor, lodger, guest, stranger.

Interpretation
This is a good time to travel for business or pleasure—perhaps even to run away from home! Get out and about and see what the world has to offer. You will need to market yourself, possibly while looking for a new job. Improve your manner and appearance, and be careful about your associates. You may be outside the normal network on a quest of your own. Be flexible and adapt to what crosses your path. Do not be afraid to act alone. Attempts to reach your destination too quickly will fail, so move slowly. Concentrate on each step before progressing to the next one.

The Lines
Lowest line
You may be behaving badly or being petty. If you go on like this you will lose what security you have. Do not make a drama out of everything.

Second line up
Take care of your property and avoid excess. Be prepared to relocate.

Third line up
Avoid being pulled into the conflict or you will be hurt. Be ready to move on and change direction.

Fourth line up
Being careless can be expensive. You may not enjoy holding yourself in check but you have no choice at the moment.

Fifth line up
You receive praise from on high. Have confidence in yourself because now you can be successful.

Top line
Stop being self-righteous. Be strong and dignified and do not put yourself down either.

57. Sun. Penetrating.
Upper trigram: Sun. Gentleness. Wind.
Lower trigram: Sun. Gentleness. Wind.

The Image
Sun is one of the eight doubled trigrams. It symbolizes wind and wood. It is associated with gentleness, so it is like a gentle breeze or a slowly growing and maturing tree.

Keywords
Enter into, put into, supple, mild, submit, be shaped by, support, base.

Interpretation
You need to persevere. Be reasonable and others will accept your ideas. Bend with the wind and do not be argumentative. You can penetrate to the core of your problem by being supple and adaptable. You may need to be humble

and to hide your virtues. Being steadfast will produce results, but do not push. Have clear objectives and act honorably to achieve success. This may be a good time for those who travel on business or need to deal with people in foreign places.

The Lines

Lowest line

Do not be so indecisive. You need to follow your decisions through. Knowing is not the same as doing.

Second line up

Get to the bottom of things and bring them out into the open. Evaluate and reevaluate.

Third line up

Do not make excessive demands of people. You can be successful so long as you keep working at it. Be decisive.

Fourth line up

All your regrets disappear. Think carefully and look before you leap. Combine modesty with action.

Fifth line up

Take some time to prepare and make sure that things are all in order. Unpleasant feelings may upset you.

Top line

You have gone too far in trying to correct things so be firm but not too hard.

58. Tui. Joy.

Upper trigram: Tui. Joyous. Lake.
Lower trigram: Tui. Joyous. Lake.

The Image

This hexagram is important, because it is one of the eight that are formed by the doubling of a trigram. It symbolizes the smiling lake and its attribute is joyousness. A lake evaporates upward and while it may dry up, when two lakes are joined they do not dry up as readily, because one replenishes the other. This suggests that knowledge should be a refreshing and vitalizing force.

Keywords

Express yourself, persuade, inspire, enjoy, interface, interact, stir up, urge on, cheer, pleasure, meet, gather, exchange, trade.

Interpretation

This is a great time for career and financial matters, especially those that involve communicating with others. Careers that rely on talking, singing, acting, teaching, or diplomacy will succeed now. Express yourself openly and interact with others. Talk, bargain, and exchange information. Inner contentment will be reflected outwardly to others and outer harmony will generate inner peace. Be humble and avoid arrogance and talking too much about your success. Your family life will improve and you will gain peace of mind.

The Lines

Lowest line

Others seem to have control over your life just now. Be content with what you already have.

Second line up

Trust your sense of purpose because other people will lead you into bad habits if you let them. Do not be drawn into activities that you believe to be wrong.

Third line up

An opportunity is coming, but it is not the right one for you. Think before making a decision.

Fourth line up

Do not let your emotions affect your judgment. Self-indulgence and sensuality are not everything.

Fifth line up
Strip away your old ideas and sort things out. Weakness will not get you very far. Stay away from dangerous situations.

Top line
Things are not clear yet. Feel good about yourself but do not get a swelled head.

59. Huan. Dispersing.
Upper trigram: Sun. Gentleness. Wind.
Lower trigram: K'an. Abyss. Water.

The Image
Wind blows over water and disperses it. This suggests that when our energy is bottled up, gentleness dissolves the blockage.

Keywords
Scatter, break up obstacles, dispel illusions, fears and suspicions, untie, dissolve resistance.

Interpretation
There may be a change of address, a new business venture, a change of job, or recovery from an illness on the way now. In some way you make a change in location. This is a great time to alter your attitudes and also to brush up your appearance. You can eliminate misunderstandings. A family may become scattered due to one or two of its members stretching their wings or moving on. Marriage and relationships will be put on the back burner for a while because you will be too busy traveling and working to concentrate on them. Follow a middle path and try not to stray far away from it if you wish to be successful. You may meet people from your past.

The Lines

Lowest line

Avoid dangerous situations. Problems should be dealt with before they become serious. If you have a good idea, act on it now.

Second line up

Remove obstacles by not relying so much on others. An inspired idea will be useful. Be fair in your judgment of others.

Third line up

Do not allow desire for a love affair or for anything else to distract you. Be an adjudicator or peacemaker.

Fourth line up

Ponder on what is truly significant for you. There is a large task ahead of you, so seek help if you need it.

Fifth line up

Your problems are all in your head; do not rush around doing things to solve them. A good idea can pull everyone together.

Top line

Remove the possibility of conflict. If a quarrel is looming, sort it out now.

60. Chieh. Limitation.

Upper trigram: K'an. Abyss. Water.
Lower trigram: Tui. Joyous. Lake.

The Image

A lake occupies a limited space, so when more water enters, it overflows. This shows that limits must be set. The image shows water below and water above, with the earth between them acting as a restriction.

Keywords
Separate, distinguish and join things, express ideas, unit of time, measure, moderate, firm, loyal, true.

Interpretation
Teamwork and self-control are needed now; this is the right time to discuss your situation with others. You need to be cautious and accept certain limitations. Reserves of energy, property, or money will be needed while you sit out a difficult situation. When doors open again you will be able to move forward, but for the time being you must follow the rules, even if they are someone else's. Do not harm yourself or others with rules that are bitter or harsh. Limitations are troublesome but they can be useful. If you live economically in normal times, you will be prepared for times of want. Stay calm, be wise, and think ahead.

The Lines
Lowest line
You have done your best; there is not much more that you can do for the time being. Stop, remain quiet, and do not step out of your familiar territory for a while.
Second line up
Do not let the opportunity for change slip through your fingers. You cannot influence others now; concentrate on changing yourself.
Third line up
If you are suffering, talk about it with others rather than bottling it up. Do not be dragged into other people's arguments.
Fourth line up
Say what you have to but do so quietly and without fuss. Concentrate on solving your current problems rather than worrying about the future.

Fifth line up
Say what you need to as nicely as possible. A split is inevitable. Do not impose restrictions on others while ignoring them yourself.
Top line
Take action before everyone and everything falls apart. Avoid being too severe toward others or telling them how bitter you are.

61. Chung Fu. Inner truth.
Upper trigram: Sun. Gentleness. Wind.
Lower trigram: Tui. Joyous. Lake.

The Image
The wind blows over the lake and stirs the water, making the surface visible. It symbolizes a breakthrough in knowledge or understanding.

Keywords
Inner, central, calm, stable, balanced, correct, mediate, intermediary, sincere, truthful, reliable, verified, have confidence.

Interpretation
Be true to yourself and sincere toward others in order to gain their trust. There will be great changes for the better in your career, business, and financial affairs as well as in matters of the heart. A change of address is possible and new scenery will be beneficial. There may be stormy weather ahead, but this is probably due to the turmoil that upheavals of this magnitude are likely to bring. Think about legal actions before getting involved; put off serious judgments. Learn to be happy with yourself and your life as you plan for the future. Material and practical issues are less important than inner peace.

The Lines

Lowest line
If you are always thinking of someone else, you will never be at ease. Get help if you need it.

Second line up
A new person comes into your life and shows you how to get exactly what you want. You are in charge of your destiny now.

Third line up
There is little that you can do in this situation. Take advice from someone in authority. Your strength lies in your relationships with others.

Fourth line up
You need to go your own way. There will be news that makes you happy or sad, and the behavior of others can affect your mood. You are not really in control.

Fifth line up
Act on your ideas. Insight will help you. You need to show the full strength of your personality.

Top line
Why go on like this? You need to concentrate on your good points.

62. Ksiao Kuo. Moderation.
Upper trigram: Chen. Arousing. Thunder.
Lower trigram: Ken. Keeping still. Mountain.

The Image
In the mountains, thunder seems much nearer. This indicates that you need to concentrate on what needs to be done and to do your duty at this time.

Keywords
Adapt to what crosses your path, reduce, lessen, go beyond, surpass, overtake, surmount.

Interpretation

Your progress will be halted, and this may be due to external forces or perhaps your own feelings of negativity or fear. Do not let bad feelings stand in your way. There is no need to be a miser, so give generously of your time and resources; you will be repaid. Do not waste your energy or get into a panic needlessly. Pay attention to detail, because success will come in small ways. Do not be overambitious, but be modest and conscientious in order to achieve results. If storms arrive, stay safe and wait for them to pass.

The Lines

Lowest line

You are overreaching yourself; you may act to your own detriment.

Second line up

Everything will go well. Be conscientious about fulfilling your responsibilities.

Third line up

You are in a perilous position; be prepared to defend yourself. You may have to change location.

Fourth line up

You should soon meet the object of your desire. Do not try to stay in the same place now that your difficulties are passing. Your fate rests in the hands of others.

Fifth line up

Extremely good luck is on the way now. You need helpers around you to complete your tasks.

Top line

Rely on yourself and do not act selfishly. Aim only as high as you need to.

63. Chi Chi. Completion.
Upper trigram: K'an. Abyss. Water.
Lower trigram: Li. Clinging. Flame.

The Image
When water hangs over fire, it generates energy. If the water boils over, the fire is extinguished and its energy is lost. If the heat is too great, the water evaporates into the air. This means that caution is needed to keep things in balance.

Keywords
Completed, finished, past, overcome, begin action, give help, bring relief, succeed, complete, achieve.

Interpretation
A cycle has ended. You should consolidate what you have achieved so far in order to build for the future. You must guard against losing all that you have gained. This is not a time to make further changes but to sit back and wait until things settle down. Gather your energy and use it effectively. Act with caution. Think deeply about your problems and prepare yourself. Marriage or a serious relationship is favorable, as you have probably passed the courtship phase.

The Lines
Lowest line
You are starting too quickly. Try to avoid reaching beyond your abilities. Do not overstep the mark.
Second line up
Do not chase what is gone; let it return of its own accord. You can succeed, with help from others. Do not try to draw too much attention to yourself.
Third line up
Do not put up with difficulties or adapt to someone else's demands even if you are weary and distressed. Keep your head down and get on with things. If you are

plagued by negative thoughts replace them with positive ones.

Fourth line up
Be on your guard. Even if you know that you are right, do not shout about it.

Fifth line up
You need to be sincere. Keep your goals reasonable and take action on the things that really matter.

Top line
You are in too deep and you are not in a position to deal with this. Do not start anything new.

64. Wei Chi. Before completion.
Upper trigram: Li. Clinging. Flame.
Lower trigram: K'an. Abyss. Water.

The Image
The flames in a fire leap upward, while water flows down, so these two opposite concepts take two different directions. If you are trying to achieve something, start by investigating the nature of the forces in question and discover their proper place.

Keywords
Incomplete, not yet, overcome obstacle, begin, give help, succeed, complete.

Interpretation
This is the start of a new phase, but you will still need to finish the project in hand. It may be necessary to revise your knowledge and to discard what you no longer need. Something new is due to come along very soon, so rest and gather your energy for this decisive fresh move. The possibilities are great, so it is time to clear the decks and to get

ready. You are following the right path, but you must avoid disputes. Success will come to you in due course.

The Lines

Lowest line
You are doing too much too soon and you do not really understand the situation. Celebrate, relax, and enjoy your achievements.

Second line up
Start slowly. You can make it if you try. The time to act has not yet come, but you need to gather your strength.

Third line up
You are preparing for a decisive new move. A struggle is inevitable but you will overcome problems.

Fourth line up
Put your ideas to the test. You have to confront your own ghosts. You will be frustrated for a while, so change directions if you can.

Fifth line up
Patience, determination, inner faith, and focusing on your goals will get you where you want to be.

Top line
Get together with others and celebrate. Do not start anything new now. Relax and enjoy what you have achieved and give all the striving and yearning a rest for a while.

Index